All About Cookies

MILK BAR

all about cookies

Christina Tosi

with Shannon Salzano

WITHDRAWN

Photographs by Henry Hargreaves

Clarkson Potter/Publishers

New York

To my mom, Greta. The woman who's
always told me my cookies were delicious,
even when they most certainly were not.

*(A mother's palate is not very discerning, but,
man, can she be one heck of a life cheerleader.)*

CONTENTS

PEP TALK

In the wild, wonderful world of dessert, possibilities are endless when you turn on the oven: crimped pie crusts when the season gives you bushels of fruit, layers of cake (unfrosted on the sides, obvi) when there's a celebration nigh. But what about all the days in between? Cookies are what I always choose. Cookies are where it all started for me.

Cookies were my first invitation into the kitchen. Cookies were the thing that inspired my first apron, my first step stool, my first mess, and, of course, my first, and perhaps greatest, food obsession.

When I was a kid, I passed on dreams of being the first female president or a prized veterinarian to dream about opening Cookies, Cookies, Cookies, my not-so-cleverly-named bakery. Cookies made my grandmothers my heroes, my best friends. Cookies were my safe place in the world in my awkward teenage years.

Cookies were the secret to living life on my terms. Decades later, not a single thing has changed.

Once I learned to follow a recipe, I made batch after batch, and then batch after batch after ditching the recipe. I experimented, asking myself, "What if I added twice the sugar? Half the flour? Double the baking soda?" As you might imagine, there were some good batches, but mostly a lot of really, really bad batches. My poor mother, Greta, would remark every time, "Ooooh. Yum!" She nibbled through each disaster after a long day's work with a big, proud smile.

I kept at it. I was happiest when my head was down, when I was lost in my own imagination, a wooden spoon and a beat-up bowl ready for magic to be made.

I took the leap to move to New York City, hone my skills, and sharpen my craft—and find direction in my life. I worked with nearly every pastry form and occupation my new home had to offer: breads, crème pâtissière, chibousts, croissants, macarons, and mignardises, plated desserts aplenty, sorbets, sundaes, soufflés, and more. I traversed every possible dessert only to find the thing I was looking for was the very thing I already knew: The answer was cookies.

It's been over twelve years since I opened Milk Bar, going from home baking twelve cookies to a batch, to industrial sheet pans yielding forty-eight cookies per bake, to now a cookie factory line that runs tens of thousands of cookies at a time. And I'm STILL just getting started.

But along the way it's always been important to refill the creativity well. Milk Bar has a roster of tried-and-trues that we've made for years: the cornflake-chocolate chip-marshmallow cookie, the compost, the confetti, the corn, the chocolate-chocolate, the blueberry and cream. If you've baked from my other books, you know my cookie past . . . you may know some of the classics from my childhood, like my mom's famous The Gretas, or my Grandma's Oatmeal Cookies. But the recipes that lie ahead of you are from my cookie *present*.

I've gone deep into our bag of tricks, brushed up on baking science, even reinvented a few of the Milk Bar classics or some of our favorite flavor stories. And what's come out is a collection of brand-new cookie recipes, ideas, and even cookie forms that I have never been more excited about.

For those of you who think a cookie is just a cookie, and all cookie cookbooks are the same, welcome, my friend, to our crazy, amazing love affair with the most unsung hero of pastry. Bake a few batches with me and, I promise, you'll never look at cookies the same way again.

PREP TALK

THE WARES

One of the most attractive attributes of cookies is that they don't require much. You just need an oven (and sometimes not even that, see page 149), a bowl, a spoon, and something to bake them on or in. This means most cookies can come together in whatever kitchen you're in. I love a good vacation rental batch of Chipless Wonders (page 128) or PB S'mores Bars (page 66). Just a step or two beyond those basics, here are a few of the things I've found over the years that help the cookie-making process go smoother.

BAKING PANS

Used for bar cookies, a pan can be either square (8 × 8-inch) or rectangular (9 × 13-inch—often called a lasagna pan). The pan has tall sides to keep the dough from spreading so that the bar cookie goes up and not out. Be mindful to use the specific size pan recommended in the recipe so you get the optimal thickness/thinness and correct bake time.

Pro tip: I order aluminum pans with lids in bulk online. One fewer thing to wash, and they make it easy to drop off treats to the team/neighbors/strangers/new friends.

BAKING SHEETS

They need not be fancy, they need not be new. I recommend a heavy-bottomed baking sheet, as it is less likely to warp. A flimsy baking sheet means some of your cookies will bake unevenly, usually burning at the bottom. At the bakery we use full-size sheet pans, as we make so many cookies at a time, but at home a regular ol' "half-sheet pan," 18 × 13 inches, is your go-to.

COOKIE SCOOPS

2¾-ounce metal scoops—or "blue scoops" as pro kitchens call them because their handles are usually blue—give the size cookie we like most: not too big, not too small, perfectly crushable. A scoop helps guarantee your cookies are the same size, which will help ensure they bake consistently.

A few cookies in this book call for a smaller scoop size for reasons unique to them. Heed this advice, as they'll bake at a different time and temperature.

OFFSET SPATULA

Not to be picture perfect or fussy, but an offset spatula can help you smooth stray bits of sandwich cookie filling or spread a layer of filling in a snap cookie. They also help for releasing and moving cookies of any kind off a baking sheet or piece of wax paper or parchment without fear of breaking.

OVEN THERMOMETER

Each oven is different. Some run hot, some cold, some inconsistently—an oven thermometer helps you hit the desired temperature, despite what the outer oven dial may say. You can usually find them in the equipment section of your grocery store. It's the best $5 to $20 you can invest in your baking future.

PARCHMENT PAPER/SILICONE BAKING MAT

Yes, the alluring premise of a quick cleanup is one big reason I use parchment paper to line my baking sheets, but it's not the only one. Parchment paper creates a layer between the baking sheet and the cookie, resulting in a more even baking surface and therefore a more even baking temperature. (Do not sub it out for aluminum foil, which will have the opposite effect.) It also makes transferring your cookies off the hot baking sheet to cool much easier.

When rolling dough for cookies, sandwiching the dough between two sheets of parchment paper is life-changing. (You will remain cool, calm, sane!)

You can think of a silicone baking mat as basically a reusable, washable piece of parchment, and they work great.

If you don't have parchment paper, hit "add to cart" for your next baking session. In the meantime coat your pan with baking spray or smother it with your leftover butter wrappers (my grandma's pro tip).

SCALE

A digital kitchen scale is another $20 investment that pays out big-time. We give you the volume (or "freedom") measurements for ease, but if you want to unleash the accuracy of your inner pro baker, using a scale is the first step. You can easily find them at your home goods store or online.

SPATULA

One big no-no in the cookie-making process: not scraping your mixing bowl to make sure all of your ingredients are getting in on the mixing action. A silicone spatula is your best friend, and make sure it's heat-resistant if you're getting into caramels and melting chocolate.

STAND MIXER

Listen, I've made a few batches of cookies in my day, and when there isn't a mixer handy, I roll up my sleeves and flex my biceps. But a stand mixer saves a lot of hassle and helps make sure every single batter and batch is completely homogenous. If there is one mistake I see more often than others in the cookie-making process, it's rushing the creaming stage—see page 20 for my TMI on creaming—and a mixer fitted with a paddle helps enormously.

TIMER

Too many a batch of cookies has been lost because someone foolishly told themselves, "I'm sure I'll know when 12 minutes is up"—trust me, you won't. I don't and I'm cookies' biggest fan! The timer on your phone works great, as does a regular kitchen timer.

THE GOODS

Baking is half science and half creativity. You know I want you to reach deep into your cupboard and your imagination to bring your YOUNESS to the recipes in this book! But the best way to tweak and tinker with a recipe successfully is to understand the role all of your ingredients play in a recipe. You have to learn the rules first before you can learn how to break them. Here's a list of what we keep on the dry storage shelves in our cookie factories and a little info about them so you can live your best rule-breaking baking life.

BAKING POWDER AND BAKING SODA

If you've ever baked before, you're familiar with these two standbys, but maybe don't know the actual role each plays. While both add a kind of flavor, tenderize texture, and help in the golden brown color department while in the oven, these leaveners primarily control the rise and spread of a cookie as it bakes. Double-acting baking powder gives your cookies lift and height—acting first when combined with a liquid, and again when it hits the heat of the oven. Baking soda also lifts (if there is an acid in the mix, like buttermilk or lemon juice) and helps your cookies spread, causing them to expand on the surface of your baking sheet.

If your cookie is too tall and not spreading enough, reduce or remove the baking powder, or add or increase the baking soda slightly, or remove a bit of the flour (just a couple tablespoons in a batch will make a difference).

If your cookie is spreading too much, reduce or remove the baking soda, add or increase the baking powder slightly, and/or add 2 to 4 tablespoons of flour.

BUTTER

I wish I could rearrange the alphabet so butter could come first in this list. This seemingly simple ingredient can make or break your baked goods. If there is one ingredient to spend a little more of your hard-earned dollars on, it's butter. You have two important choices to make:

Unsalted: Save the salted butter for your dinner table. Using unsalted butter allows you to control the salt level of your recipe. It's easy to add salt, but impossible to subtract.

European-style: Made from cultured dairy, this style of butter has a deeper flavor compared to the generic stuff. It's also higher in fat—typically 82% or more—and fat equals flavor. We like Plugra best.

You also have to know that butter isn't just about flavor in your baked goods! Creaming it well is a key step to success. See Yes, Creaming Is That Important (page 20) for more.

CHOCOLATE

The higher the percentage on the package label, the more cocoa the chocolate contains, compared to milk solids, sugars, or other ingredients. In other words, the more intense the chocolate flavor. On the lowest percentage end of the spectrum, white and then milk chocolate are sweeter, more mellow, and least intense in chocolate flavor. Semisweet lives somewhere in the middle, then bittersweet, then the dark chocolates clock in at 65%, 70%, and sometimes higher percentages for maximum chocolate intensity. I'll specify which to use per recipe—just know that you can adjust it how you want it by swapping chocolate types, either going a bit more intense and bitter, or sweeter and more mellow.

White chocolate: TBH it's not even technically chocolate because it contains no cocoa solids, only cocoa butter. We use it to enrobe Snaps (page 160), to add creaminess to a flavor story (Cereal Milk Cream Soda Cookies, page 96), and to help set a glaze or enhance mouthfeel. Whatever white chocolate form you can get your hands on (chips, bars, pistoles, et al.) works just fine.

CITRIC ACID

Available widely online or as vitamin C powder in the vitamin aisle, this acid is used to enhance the flavor in many of our citrus-based recipes. Pucker up, a little goes a long way!

COCOA POWDER

We can be fussy about cocoa powder, but the recipes in this book have all been developed with good ol' Hershey's, because I wasn't going to send you on a Valrhona goose chase just to make a killer cookie at home.

CORN POWDER

Freeze-dried corn kernels ground into a flour-like consistency, this is a powerhouse ingredient. It is the hard-to-put-your-finger-on flavor in our Milk Bar Pie filling and Cereal Milk Soft Serve. This golden powder brings a fresh and natural depth to recipes. When we call for it we mean it, so if you are serious, grab some freeze-dried corn from Whole Foods and get to pulverizing it in a blender, and make sure to store it in an airtight container.

DULCE DE LECHE

Creamy, dreamy, this caramelized milk is a way of life. It's thicker and more luxurious than regular caramel, because it has milk as its base rather than water. You can find it in cans in the international aisle or at a Latin supermarket—La Lechera brand is our go-to.

You can also DIY by simmering an unopened can of sweetened condensed milk, label removed, fully submerged in a pot of water for 2 hours. Double, triple, quadruple also work; just make sure the water level is always 2 inches above the can—to remove risk of explosion and bodily harm. Cool the can completely before opening, or another in-your-face explosion could occur.

EGGS

Eggs play a huge role in baking, bringing structure, hydration, texture, and flavor to your cookies. Most people don't realize eggs come in varying sizes, but bakers know that a little difference can really affect how your recipe bakes. We always use "large" eggs in our recipes; the large eggs you would find in your grocery store will work just fine.

EXTRACTS

Liquid extracts help impart certain flavors without messing up the water content, which would affect the science of baking in a recipe. We try to avoid using them as a crutch—there are a lot of ways to bring flavor and life into a recipe, and when we call for an extract it's probably because we needed the oomph that the ingredient couldn't deliver on its own.

Vanilla extract: Available everywhere, this is the vanilla you know and love. It has a dark vanilla color and scent, and is awesome in almost any baked good—not to impart a vanilla taste per se, but to round out and enliven other flavors in a recipe. Try a chocolate chip cookie without vanilla extract and you'll see what I mean. McCormick will always do right by us.

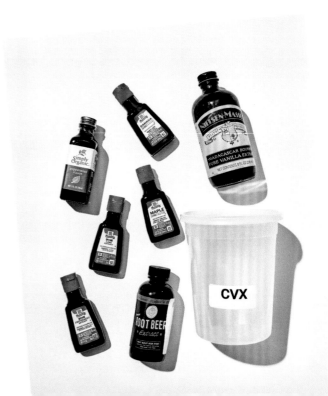

Clear vanilla extract: On the opposite side of the coin, clear vanilla extract brings the edgy, crisp sweetness you instinctively relate to creamy, dreamy birthdays, as it's used in store-bought box cake mixes and frostings. It tugs on our nostalgia in a very specific, irreplaceable way. Most grocery stores don't have this variety, so you may need to shop online. DO NOT substitute regular vanilla extract for it; it is a vastly different flavor experience.

Banana, butter, lemon, and peppermint extracts: Most grocery stores carry these extracts and a few others, though you can never go wrong buying them online either. One word of caution: When shopping for peppermint extract (candy cane mint), be careful not to confuse it with just "mint" extract (short for "spearmint") or you'll end up with toothpaste-tasting Grasshopper Pie Bars (page 82).

FLOURS

Flour gives structure to your cookies, plain and simple.

All-purpose flour: Ninety-nine percent of the recipes in this book use all-purpose flour—so much so that we just call it "flour." Any brand will do, though we like King Arthur. Its middle-ground protein content (versus a higher percentage of protein in bread flour, or a lower percentage in cake flour) is more dependable in the mixing process—translation: Your cookies are less likely to get tough and glutinous or overly fluffy.

Corn flour: Unsurprisingly, swapping out some all-purpose flour for corn flour helps baked goods taste corny.

Gluten-free flour: Bob's Red Mill or Cup4Cup work great.

FOOD COLORING

Facts are facts, and not every baked good's natural color scheme matches the flavor story your eyes are expecting. We don't go wild on food coloring, but when we want Nana Nillas (page 135) to be the calm yellow color of our dreams, we add a few drops of coloring. If it's not your jam, skip it, but don't say I didn't warn you.

FRUIT

More specifically: dried fruit. Fresh or frozen fruit can mess with the water content of your recipe and spell major disaster for a butter-bound creation. Dried fruit brings the fun without the moisture and is your best route for delivering on flavor and texture. Always check the ingredient label before buying to make sure you're getting the fruit in its truest form (anything that lists sugar or preservatives will mute the fruit flavor you're depending on).

NONFAT MILK POWDER

Often labeled as instant nonfat dry milk, this white powder adds chew and oomph to any baked good it touches. If it's not in the baking aisle, you can often find it near the drink powders or sometimes in the baby food aisle. If you want to fully understand its secret powers, try a side-by-side taste of a recipe without it and you'll get what I am saying.

OIL

When called for, oil can help with tenderness and moisture in a cookie. Unless we're looking for its flavor to play a role (Hello, Donut Wafers, page 190), a neutral, odorless, and flavorless oil like grapeseed, canola, or vegetable will do you right. In this book we also call for oil as a partner to chocolate, helping it stay smooth when melted for coatings.

SALT

Salt has an important role in baking. It helps create a bridge for flavors, to bring dynamism to a recipe's taste. First thing first: We use kosher salt. It's not iodized and has larger granules than table salt. Our preferred brand is Diamond Crystal, and our recipes are tested with it. Be warned: Morton brand kosher salt is about 66 percent heavier by volume than Diamond Crystal kosher salt, and doesn't incorporate as easily, leaving your baked goods feeling too salty in some bites and underbalanced in others. If you're weighing your salt, you don't need to sweat it, but if you're using volume measurements, just know that you will need about half the volume of salt in the recipe if you're using Morton kosher salt.

SUGAR

Generally, my cookie recipes call for "sugar," by which we mean granulated sugar, the regular everyday stuff.

Light/dark brown sugar: Some recipes need a deeper flavor to go with sweetness, in which case we swap out a percentage of the white stuff for light brown sugar (and rarely, dark brown sugar for even more depth). Largely in Cookieland, granulated, light brown, and dark brown sugars are interchangeable depending on your flavor vision. If you want your Chipless Wonders (page 128) to be deeper and more sultry, swap out some or all of the granulated sugar in the recipe for light brown.

Confectioners' sugar: Confectioners' sugar, aka powdered sugar, aka 10X (a reference to the fact that it is granulated sugar that has been ground down ten times finer than the original granules) is used in glazes and frostings when you need the sugar to completely dissolve into the mixture. It usually has a tiny pinch of cornstarch in it, too, to keep it from clumping up on you.

Turbinado sugar: Similar to the textural finish and visual wow a flaky sea salt adds to the top of a cookie, this rough, golden sugar adds mouthfeel and extra finishing sweetness to a recipe. It may be called Sugar in the Raw on your grocery shelf.

REAL TALK

As much as I want you to let your freak flag fly in the kitchen, there are a few lessons I've learned over the years that can save you a lot of heartache as you find your voice. Most cookie flops can be traced back to one of these baking basics, so before you get after it, take a beat to learn the unbreakable rules of the road (which are in the order of business from start to finish).

GREAT IN, GREAT OUT

Great ingredients in the bowl mean great baked goods out of the oven. It stands to reason that if butter is the cornerstone of your recipe, for instance, you want to work with the good stuff. Same goes with chocolate, honey, spices—use stuff that tastes good to you from the jump. Great flavor in the form of great ingredients ensures great flavor out of every batch of cookies you bake. I don't make the rules, I just call them like I see them.

DON'T SKIP THE LEAVENERS.
AND DON'T YOU DARE SKIP THE SALT.

We've all had the moment as we gather up ingredients, excited to get baking, and notice we're out of either baking powder or baking soda, and reason with ourselves that one or two teaspoons can't be THAT important, can it? It can and it is. Those pinches of white powders are what we call chemical leavening agents—and they produce gas (the good kind) within your cookie. Without those small amounts of baking powder and/or baking soda your cookies will end up flat. As much as it might pain you to do so, hold off on your baking sesh until you have these MVPs in hand.

Speaking of MVPs, the Grand Slam ingredient in EVERY. SINGLE. RECIPE is salt. We don't use salt to make things salty—rather, salt deepens, extends, and rounds the flavor of every recipe in this book. Think of it as a sharpener, an amplifier of any flavor you aspire to bake. A little salt is like listening to a great song on full blast.

BREAK OUT THE SCALE

I've already given you a scale on the list of tools that will help your cookies turn out incredible every time, but it bears expounding on. Much as no two snowflakes

are the same, no two measured cups of flour are either. What? Yep, no one ever tells you this stuff! My 1 cup of flour might weigh in at 150 grams, yours might be a scant 132 grams. These small differences can add up to big mistakes when you are trying to get all the ingredients to work in harmony. So why guess?! Crack out your scale, tare it to zero, and bake with the peace of mind that you're nailing the measurements each and every time. In these recipes I do list the volume measurement for each weight, because not having a scale handy shouldn't keep you from having a blast in the kitchen. (Plus I don't pack a scale when I bake on vacation :)) But if you want your recipe to come out the way it did when we wrote it, use a scale.

ROLL CALL: ORDER MATTERS

I stand before you, vowing to always save you time when possible. Cutting out the fuss is my way of life. If your cookies could turn out 100 percent delicious by mixing everything together at once, I would be the first one to let you know, but the reality is: When there is an order listed, it's because it matters. Baking is sometimes a fickle chemistry experiment, and each step is carefully building bonds and creating reactions. Adding baking soda too early can result in cookies that don't spread. Tossing your vanilla extract in at the last minute could mean it doesn't distribute evenly. To drive this point home, we always list the ingredients in the order you will use them. Our pro move is to stick a piece of removable kitchen (painter's) tape next to the recipe, checking off each ingredient as it goes in to make triple dog sure that you got it all in.

YES, CREAMING IS THAT IMPORTANT

You might feel that 5/6/10 minutes is a very long time to be mixing butter and sugar(s) together, as you give me the side-eye and stare at your mixer, impatiently longing for a batch of pretzel cookies to be done. And you know what, it is! But it's crucial for getting a flavor-packed, well-baked, perfectly textured cookie. Basically, when we mix the butter and sugar with the paddle for these periods of time, we are forcing ingredients that don't want to be together to be best friends. They are reluctant at first, but over time the mixing forces a strong emulsifying bond and the two combine into one flavorful mix.

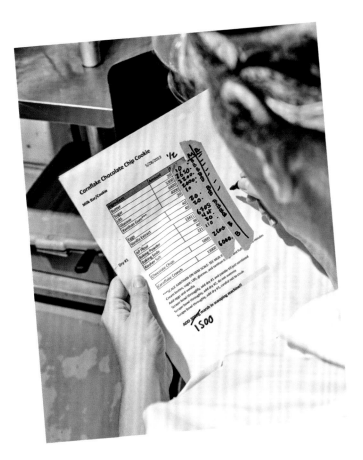

Because we are overachievers, our recipes force more butter and sugar together than other recipes you might have come across, which is why these cookies are so exceptional. If you don't get the butter and sugar to bond strongly, you will end up with a flat cookie, or a cookie with pools of butter or craggly edges. My suggestion is to set a timer for however long the recipe instructs your creaming to go for to keep yourself honest. Have an impromptu dance party, do a quick meditation, chug a glass of water with that free time. One bite of your perfect pretzel cookie and you will know those extra minutes in the mixer were worth it.

DO NOT BE A SIR MIX-A-LOT

When it's time to add the dry ingredients, I repeat again and again to "mix just until the dough comes together, no longer than 1 minute." You're probably saying "Tosi—we get it!" I'm here to set you up for ultimate cookie success, and this lesson is a big one. Similar to properly creaming the butter and sugar, properly mixing your dough is something you need to keep your eye on. You want to mix the dry ingredients into the butter/sugar/egg combo for as short a time as possible. Once that mixer starts going, the gluten clock starts ticking: The longer you mix, the more gluten is developing in your cookie, and the more gluten, the more rocky, tight, and bready your cookies will be. No offense to bread, but I want my dense and fudgy cookie to be buttery, soft, and tender (with some crisp on the edge), so I mix my flour and other dry ingredients in as little as I can while ensuring they're well distributed.

It's also worth flagging that if your recipe has inclusions—chocolate chips, sprinkles, etc.— you want to ease up even further on this mixing moment, taking your dough to a shaggy texture once you add the flour and other dry ingredients, accounting for the additional time you will need to get the inclusions mixed in.

GAME PAUSED

There are situations in which we might ask you to hit *pause* before your cookies go into the oven.

Your butter needs time to chill. All that delicious fat we worked so hard to get into your cookie dough may still want to escape. Chilling your dough for an hour (or sometimes longer) before baking it allows the fat to firm up and strengthen its bond with sugars even further, meaning it will not run the risk of melting and spreading out as the cookie bakes. If you find your cookies are spreading too much in the oven, it may mean your butter was too warm or the bond with the sugars not strong enough. An hour in the fridge or, even better, freezer will set you up for success.

Your flour needs time to hydrate and/or relax. Though we don't TMI you on this in specific recipes, allowing the dough to rest in recipes like Chocolate Babka Cookies (page 216) gives the flour a chance to hydrate and relax before going for another rolling session. Without this pause, the dough will be resistant.

Now you know why the prebake pause is called for, so please don't skip it.

TESTING, TESTING

How awesome would it be if you had a crystal ball that would show you exactly how your cookies will turn out every single time before you take the batch out of the oven? Great news: You do! Let me intro you real quick to your new BFF: the tester cookie (TC). This sacrificial lamb is the single cookie you scoop and bake solo, before you commit to scooping and baking the whole batch. This lone soldier's mission is to gather information and to report back to his squad, informing them on things like:

Flavor—Want a tad more edgy by way of salt? More chocolate chips? More pb vibes?

Oven temp—You can't always trust the dial on your oven.

Evenness—Does your oven have hot or cold spots? Is your baking sheet sitting level? Does your baking sheet need a turn and rotation front to back and top rack to bottom to ensure a perfect bake?

Inclusion dispersion—Too many marshmallows in the dough but not enough in this one cookie?

Bake time—Did you make smaller/larger cookies that need less/more time in the oven? Or like a slightly longer bake and less fudgy center?

When your TC comes out of the oven, you are given a second chance at life, and can adjust your dough recipe, mixing time, or baking procedure to ensure the rest of the team bakes perfectly.

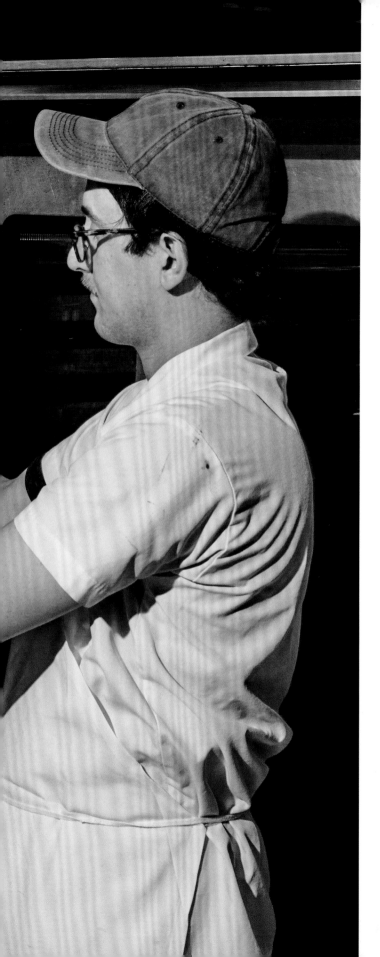

AND IN CASE YOU NEED A LITTLE BOOST

If I had one message for grade-school Christina making a mess of her kitchen in the joyful pursuit of discovery, it would be: Get comfy with failure, sister.*

Nine times out of ten your brilliant new idea for a cookie is going to turn out burnt or bland or just plain yucky. Sometimes they won't even turn out at all! You'll probably feel like turning in your apron and finding a new way to spend your time. But when the puzzle seems uncrackable and you're on batch 101 of a seemingly endless journey, you'll have a eureka moment, finding just the thing you need to make cookie magic. All the wasted time and butter will be worth it, and crazily enough, it won't feel like time wasted at all because you were on your way to something special. Failures and rough drafts and works in progress are all necessary parts of creating something that is new, that is yours and yours alone.

I share my recipes because I want to invite you all into that 2 a.m. moment in my kitchen when I know I've landed on something special—when I say "This is it" as I go for another scoopful of dough or a cookie warm out of the oven. But more than that, I want you to find those moments for yourself. Yes, the recipes on these pages will result in something I believe to be pretty darn incredible, but that's where my story stops and yours starts, my friend. Mix it up! If you think the Sugar Sugar Cookies (page 104) would be awesome with some peppermint, go for it. Those shortcake crumbs from the Cherry Pie Cookies (page 118) calling to you as you start a batch of Party Bars (page 85)? Do it: no risk, no reward! A few burnt batches and some wasted flour is a whole lot better than a life full of what-ifs, so color outside the lines. Learn the rules so you can discover how you like to break them. Don't let a little fear of failure stop you from your cookie destiny. Know that I am cheering you on every step of the way.

* If I had two messages, the second would be: It's time to stop your mom from cutting your hair with a bowl as her guide.

SANDIES
& SAMMIES

Potato Chip
Shorties
32

Black
Sesame
Sandies
35

Pistachio
Fingers
57

Dulce de
Leche
Lofthouses
41

PB
Sandies
28

Triscuit
Sandies
53

Brown
Butter
Nillas
37

Jelly Donut
Cookie
Sammies
31

Cheez-
Grits
58

Gooey
Butter
Cookies
54

Chewy
Chocolate
Banana
Sammies
42

Lime
Ritzies
49

Fluffernutters
45

SAMMIES ARE ALL ABOUT THE BRILLIANT REALIZATION THAT IF YOU sandwich two cookies together with something sweet in the middle, nothing bad could possibly happen.

And sandies (with their cousins, the shorties) are all about the notion that oftentimes simplicity yields the best results.

Okay, but what the heck is a sandie? Sandies actually trace their heritage back to the French shortbread sablé cookie—sablé meaning "sandy" in French. In American baking, we typically sub out some of the flour in a classic shortbread cookie for another ingredient, such as ground pecans. Shortbread is delicious, but this idea of partial ingredient substitution leaves the door wide open for curiosity, flavor, and fun. I've taken the journey down several sandie roads and come up with my favorite combos for this delightfully crumbly, wonderfully coarse cookie format. (Also, shout-out to all the other brilliant countries that make their own version of a sandie—also known as polvorón in Spain, Latin America, and the Philippines, to name a few.)

In my mind anything can be made into a sammie. I mean, if you have a jar of Nutella and cookies looking at you longingly, why not? Only you know I'm going to get geeky and take it as far as I can.

PB SANDIES

Makes 18 cookies · GF

Do you remember the early days of quarantine when toilet paper was scarce and yeast was worth its weight in gold? When the lines for the supermarket snaked around the corner and flour was nowhere to be found, I wanted to develop a recipe for the folks who didn't have access to industrial-size rolling bins of flour like I do. My grandmothers are real waste-not-want-not types, so I looked in my pantry of random half-boxes of things through their eyes, and it hit me. I don't need "flour" … I can use anything that I can grind into a flour-like state and just substitute! (It's how we riffed on a sugar cookie with freeze-dried corn to make Milk Bar's corn cookies.) Once I narrowed in on Rice Krispies as my "flour," peanut butter was a natural flavor direction, and these salty-sweet babes were born. Spoiler alert—they're also accidentally gluten-free!

→ Rice Krispies aren't the only thing you can grind down—cookies, nuts, pretzels, oats, other cereal—the sky's the limit!

→ If you're a more-is-more person, go the thumbprint route—use a clean thumb to imprint into the dough round, then fill the empty space with MORE peanut butter! Technically that would make this a sandie-open-faced sammie, which is my kind of meta.

260g	creamy peanut butter	1 cup
225g	light brown sugar	1 cup (packed)
113g	unsalted butter, softened	1 stick (8 T)
1	large egg	
8g	vanilla extract	2 tsp
210g	Rice Krispies, ground to a flour	2 cups (ground)
3g	kosher salt	¾ tsp
3g	baking soda	½ tsp
2g	baking powder	½ tsp

1. Heat the oven to 350°F. Pan-spray or line two half-sheet pans with parchment paper or silicone baking mats.

2. In the bowl of a stand mixer fitted with the paddle attachment, cream together the peanut butter, brown sugar, and butter on medium-high for 2 to 3 minutes until well combined. Scrape down the sides of the bowl, add the egg and vanilla, and beat until smooth, about 1 minute.

3. Add the Rice Krispies flour, salt, baking soda, and baking powder and paddle on low speed just until the dough comes together, no longer than 1 minute. Scrape down the sides of the bowl with a spatula.

4. Using a 2¾-ounce cookie scoop (or a ⅓-cup measure), scoop the dough onto the prepared pans 2 to 3 inches apart. Flatten the domed tops with your palm (it will be a bit sticky, don't worry).

5. Bake at 350°F until golden, 10 to 12 minutes.

6. Let the cookies cool briefly on the pans, then transfer cookies to a plate or an airtight container for storage. At room temperature, the cookies will keep fresh for 3 days; in the freezer, they will keep for 1 month.

PB Sandies

JELLY DONUT COOKIE SAMMIES

Makes 18 cookies

Sometimes, even the most basic ingredients have an opportunity to contribute to the flavor story or, in this case, drive it. Leftover fryer oil (the oil we cool down, strain, and save after frying something) is pretty common in my household (please, no judgment). After a couple of batches of cannoli or funnel cakes, I have a healthy stash of this flavorful, fried-food-flavored oil ready to live a second life. When donuts were tossed out during a cookie brainstorming session at work, I knew it was that oil's time to shine. You'll be seriously amazed at how much these cookies really taste like a jelly donut!

→ If you are more of a glazed donut fan, I feel you. Turn to page 261 to read up on our favorite ways to glaze—it really depends what kind of jelly donut you love best!

→ See Upcycled Fryer Oil (page 174) for our suggestions on what you can fry up to get your fried-oil stash.

1 recipe	Donut Wafer dough (page 190)	
	flour, for rolling out	
252g	jelly of your choice	1 cup
	confectioners' sugar, for dusting	

1. Heat the oven to 325°F. Pan-spray two half-sheet pans.

2. Roll the dough out onto a clean, lightly floured surface and use a rolling pin to smooth to a ¼-inch thickness.

3. Use a large (about 4-inch) round cookie cutter to cut as many rounds as possible (you can always re-use the dough scraps, too). Then use a small (about 2-inch) round cookie cutter to cut small circles out of the inside of the large rounds so you are left with O-shaped rounds. Use a flat spatula to transfer all the rounds to the prepared sheets.

4. Bake at 325°F until golden brown around the edges, about 10 minutes. Cool completely on the pans.

5. Load the jelly into a zip-seal bag or piping bag and cut a tiny hole in one end. On half of the cookies, trace a solid line of jelly around the inner and outer edges of the donut shape to form a sort of "retaining wall." Then fill in the center of the cookies (between the jelly borders) with a light coating of jelly. Top with the remaining half of the cookies.

6. Dust the cookie sandwiches with a little confectioners' sugar and serve. Store in an airtight container at room temperature for up to 5 days.

POTATO CHIP SHORTIES

Makes 12 cookies

Just like people, every cookie has a unique personality. Some are sweet, and some, my friends, are salty. These cookies, along with their BFFs, Crunchy Corn Cookies (page 230), toe the line of how salty-sweet a cookie can be. And they are one gorgeously flavored cookie, I tell you. In true sandie formulation, subbing out some of the flour for crushed potato chips gives the cookies edge and grit and will have even the most dessert-skeptical folks out there asking for seconds.

113g	unsalted butter, softened	1 stick (8 T)
100g	sugar	½ cup
110g	flour	¾ cup
50g	potato chips, crushed	2 cups
4g	kosher salt	1 tsp
	flour, for dusting	
	sugar, for coating	

1. Heat the oven to 350°F. Pan-spray or line two half-sheet pans with parchment paper or silicone baking mats.

2. In the bowl of a stand mixer fitter with the paddle attachment, cream together the butter and sugar on medium-high for 2 to 3 minutes until smooth. Scrape down the sides of the bowl.

3. Add the flour, potato chips, and salt and mix on low just until the dough comes together.

4. Lightly dust a work surface with flour. Turn the dough onto the surface and form into a log about 6 inches long. Wet the log with a tiny amount of water and roll it in sugar to coat.

5. Roll the log in plastic wrap and refrigerate until well chilled and firm, at least 20 minutes. You want it to be sliceable without losing shape.

6. Slice the shorties into ½-inch-thick rounds and arrange on the baking sheets ½ inch apart.

7. Bake at 350°F until the edges are golden brown, 12 to 17 minutes.

8. Cool completely on the pans before serving. Store in an airtight container at room temperature for 4 to 5 days.

Potato Chip Shorties

BLACK SESAME SANDIES

Makes 48 cookies

Aside from using sesame oil in my savory cooking, I hadn't paid much mind to sesame for most of my life other than enjoying some seeds atop my hamburger bun. That is, until I had a fortuitous brush with the sesame-bomb known as halva—accidentally/fatefully grabbing a block when I meant to snatch a candy bar—and fell deeply in love. Then sesame, ground to a paste in the form of tahini, became a go-to ingredient in my baking and opened a whole world of nutty flavor to me. These sesame sandies carry that sesame love into Cookieland. A drizzle of sesame oil in the dough adds yet another sesame dimension, and we are in business.

→ If white sesame seeds are all you got, no worries! The flavor will be different, but they will work in the recipe interchangeably.

→ Clarified butter makes the richest, sandiest, most tender shortbread cookies around, since removing milk solids from the butter also removes most of the water content. Less water and more butterfat is a one-way ticket to flavor!

282g	unsalted butter	2½ sticks (20 T)
400g	sugar	2 cups, divided
6g	toasted sesame oil	1½ tsp
3g	kosher salt	¾ tsp + more for decorating
110g	black sesame seeds	¾ cup
290g	flour	2 cups

1. In a small pot, melt the butter over low heat. Remove from the heat and set aside undisturbed for 5 minutes to settle.

2. Use a spoon to skim off the milk solids (white foam) from the surface of the butter. Get as much as you can, but no need to be painstaking. Carefully pour the remaining clarified butter into a cup measure, leaving behind the buttermilk that has collected on the bottom. You should have about 1 cup of clarified butter.

3. In a bowl, combine the clarified butter, 200g (1 cup) of the sugar, the sesame oil, and salt in a bowl and set in the fridge to chill until solid, about 20 minutes.

4. Heat the oven to 350°F. Line a half-sheet pan with parchment paper.

5. In a food processor or blender, grind the sesame seeds into a rough meal. Transfer to the lined pan and toast until aromatic and nutty, about 10 minutes. Set aside to cool and turn off the oven.

6. Scrape the solidified butter/sugar mixture into a stand mixer fitted with the whisk. Whip on medium-high for 4 minutes until light and fluffy.

7. Unhook the mixing bowl from the stand mixer and add the flour and ground sesame seeds. Firmly knead the dough together by hand until crumbly but evenly mixed.

8. Divide the dough in half. Place each half on a large piece of plastic wrap. Fold the wrap over the dough and squeeze and mold it into a compact log about 2 inches wide and 6 inches long. Refrigerate until firm, a minimum of 2 hours.

9. About 20 minutes before baking, heat the oven to 350°F. Line two sheet pans with parchment paper.

(recipe continues)

10. Remove one log from the refrigerator and use your sharpest knife to cut it into ¼-inch-thick slices. Press any broken slices back together and place on the lined pan, 1 inch apart. Repeat with the other log.

11. Bake at 350°F until the cookies appear dry on top without developing any color, about 15 minutes.

12. Meanwhile, stir together the remaining 200g (1 cup) sugar and 3 finger pinches of kosher salt.

13. Let the cookies cool for 10 minutes on the pans. Then carefully coat each cookie all the way around in the sugar/salt mixture.

14. Store in an airtight container. At room temperature, the cookies will keep fresh for 3 days. The dough logs can be refrigerated for up to 3 days and frozen for 1 month.

BROWN BUTTER NILLAS

Makes about 18 cookies

When planning the recipe calendar for my Bake Club, I often go back to the drawing board on the classic, undeniably delicious, sure-to-please-a-crowd desserts. Everything from Fruit Roll-Ups to hand pies is fair game as long as it tugs at the right heartstrings. One such idea led me back to a grocery store classic: Nilla wafers. I have memories of eating these delights at friends' houses. (No way I was asking Greta to buy me some! Her response was always, "We don't buy things we know how to make.") I was too slow to realize I should have just engaged her in a recipe testing session, because though we knew how to make some killer cookies, we darn well didn't know how to make Nilla wafers.

So a few decades later, I set out to do just that. Only I discovered that the 'nilla part was waiting to be deepened by one of my favorite flavor tools, brown butter, which also happens to amp up the sandie vibes in all the right ways.

→ Use brown butter in place of regular butter in Chipless Wonders (page 128) or any other recipe where you think the depth of nuttiness will do you right.

→ This recipe calls for two half-sheet pans of the same size. The weight and conductivity of the second pan keeps the Nillas flat and caramelized all over—it's a really fun trick!

56g	Brown Butter (recipe follows), cooled	¼ cup
70g	sugar	⅓ cup
1	large egg yolk	
12g	vanilla extract	1 T
95g	flour	⅔ cup
1g	kosher salt	¼ tsp
0.5g	baking powder	⅛ tsp

1. Heat the oven to 300°F. Pan-spray or line a half-sheet pan with parchment paper or a silicone baking mat. Grab a second half-sheet pan, flip it upside down, pan-spray its bottom (alternatively, cut a piece of parchment or grab another silicone baking mat), and put it to the side.

2. In the bowl of a stand mixer fitted with the paddle attachment, cream together the brown butter and sugar on medium-high until smooth, about 30 seconds. On low speed, add the egg yolk and vanilla, and paddle until smooth. Add the flour, salt, and baking powder and mix just until combined, no more than 30 seconds.

3. Roll the dough into a log about 1 inch in diameter. Roll the log in plastic wrap and refrigerate until well chilled and firm, about 20 minutes. You want it to be sliceable without losing shape.

4. Slice the Nillas into ¼-inch-thick rounds and arrange on the first sheet pan ½ inch apart.

5. Cover the first sheet pan with the second prepped sheet pan, so that the bottom of the top sheet pan is pressing on the cookies, weighting them down.

6. Bake at 300°F until golden brown, about 18 minutes.

7. Cool completely on the pan before noshing or storing. If you have the willpower, wait for tomorrow—they're even better on day 2!

(recipe continues)

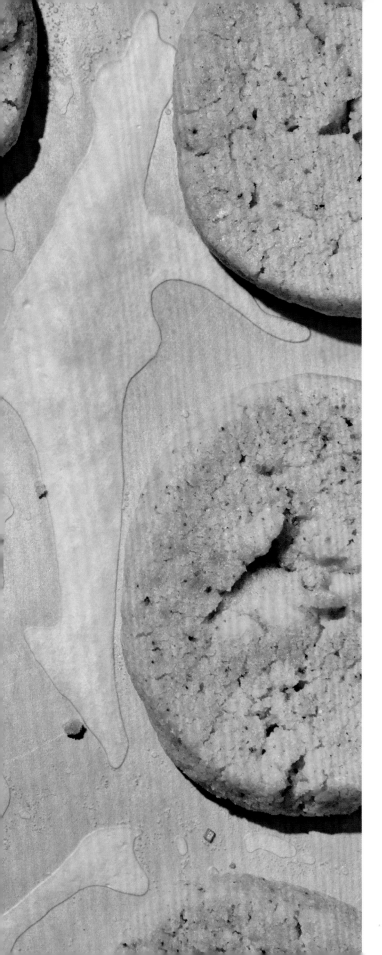

BROWN BUTTER

Makes 452g (1 pound)

Brown butter is a way of life and one of the most delicious things to use in any recipe to deepen anything with nutty, cinnamon-y, or brown-sugary flavors. Browning butter is a snap, so here is my foolproof method (you're gonna want to write this down).

452g	unsalted butter	4 sticks (1 lb)

1. In a large saucepan—I mean it, large!—melt the butter over medium-high heat. Then reduce the heat to medium-low and keep an eye on it until it reaches a deep brown color and gives off a nutty aroma, about 5 minutes. Don't be bashful now, color equals flavor, so let that butter go until you see that brown. Once you've got it (or when you're just too terrified to continue), transfer the butter to a heatproof bowl and stir to distribute the milk solids evenly.

2. Store in an airtight container in the fridge for up to 1 month.

DULCE DE LECHE LOFTHOUSES

Makes about 18 cookies

An open-faced sammie cookie, this recipe is a mash-up of a local favorite and global flair—borrowing from two of our all-time cookie heroes: alfajores and Lofthouse cookies. Varieties of alfajores exist all over Latin America, southern Europe, and the Philippines, typically comprising crumbly butter cookies sandwiching a thick spread of dulce de leche (caramelized sweetened condensed milk; see page 14) and a coating of shredded coconut. Closer to home for me, Lofthouse cookies are an American grocery store phenom: soft and cakey vanilla cookies topped with radioactive sweet pink icing and sprinkles, way more delicious than anyone would expect them to be. This recipe brings these two together for a fluffy, caramelly experience.

→ Cream cheese is a baking MVP ingredient in this recipe—a natural thickener that adds a rich depth and tangy dairy flavor while keeping the cookie soft and fluffy for many days.

→ Dulce de leche is pure gold and improves anything it touches. Stir it into black coffee. Spread it on buttered toast. Make the Milk Bar dulce de leche cake. The options are endless! See page 14 for our go-to DIY move.

200g	sugar	1 cup
113g	unsalted butter, softened	1 stick (8 T)
113g	cream cheese, softened	4 oz
1	large egg	
4g	vanilla extract	1 tsp
180g	flour	1¼ cups
5g	cornstarch	2 tsp
5g	kosher salt	1¼ tsp, divided
2g	baking powder	½ tsp
90g	desiccated coconut	1 cup
380g	dulce de leche	13 oz (1 can)

1. Heat the oven to 350°F. Pan-spray two half-sheet pans and line with parchment paper.

2. In the bowl of a stand mixer fitted with the paddle attachment, cream together the sugar, butter, and cream cheese on medium speed for 2 to 3 minutes until well combined. Scrape down the sides of the bowl, add the egg and vanilla, and beat until smooth.

3. In a medium bowl, whisk together the flour, cornstarch, 3g (¾ teaspoon) of the salt, and the baking powder to break up any lumps. Add to the mixer and paddle on low speed until just combined. It should resemble a cake batter more than a dough.

4. Using a ¾-ounce cookie scoop (1½ tablespoons), scoop the batter onto the lined pans 2 to 3 inches apart.

5. Bake at 350°F until the tops are dry, 12 to 14 minutes. The cookies should stay white on top and be lightly golden brown underneath.

6. Let the cookies cool on the pans for 10 minutes. Meanwhile, in a small bowl, stir the coconut and remaining 2g (½ teaspoon) of salt together.

7. Scoop a generous 1 teaspoon of dulce de leche on top of each cookie and use a small offset spatula or butter knife to spread it across the top, leaving a ¼-inch border around the edge. Gently press the cookie facedown into the coconut topping and swirl around to cover.

8. Transfer the cookies to a plate or an airtight container for storage. At room temperature, the cookies will keep fresh for 3 days.

CHEWY CHOCOLATE BANANA SAMMIES

Makes about 12 sammies · GF

One of the ultimate joys in being an aunt is getting to eat like a kid whenever my nieces come to visit. Okay, who am I kidding, I eat like a kid when they aren't around, too. Still, their favorite combo is banana and chocolate (usually with peanut butter not too far behind) and I'm happy to indulge when the craving calls. The dream team of a plucky, yellow, silky smooth banana buttercream lovingly sandwiched by two craggy, lighter-than-air chocolate cookies pleases this crowd of choco-nana heads every time.

→ Yes, these cookies slay with their banana buttercream buddy, but they deliver as a solo artist as well.

300g	confectioners' sugar	2½ cups
45g	cocoa powder	½ cup
4g	kosher salt	1 tsp
2	large egg whites	
8g	vanilla extract	2 tsp
1 recipe	Banana Buttercream (recipe follows)	

1. In the bowl of a stand mixer fitted with the paddle attachment, mix together the confectioners' sugar, cocoa powder, kosher salt, egg whites, and vanilla on medium until a smooth, thick dough forms. There won't seem like enough liquid at first, but continue to mix and stir until the ingredients hydrate fully.

2. Cover the dough with plastic wrap directly on its surface and refrigerate for 30 minutes.

3. Heat the oven to 350°F. Pan-spray or line two half-sheet pans with parchment paper or silicone baking mats.

4. Use a tablespoon to portion half the dough (around 12 cookies) onto a prepared pan. It's important to note that these cookies require full heat circulation in the oven and can only be baked one pan at a time! Re-cover the remainder of the dough and refrigerate until ready to use.

5. Wet your hands and very lightly round each portioned cookie into a ball and place 3 inches apart on the pan.

6. Bake at 350°F until puffed and crackly on top, 9 to 10 minutes. It's better to err on the side of underbaking than overbaking these for the sake of maximum chewiness!

7. Let the cookies cool completely on the pan. Carefully slide an offset spatula under each cookie to help release it from the pan.

8. Repeat the portioning, rounding, and baking process with the second half of the dough.

9. Pair off the cookies by size. Flip one cookie per pair upside down so the flattest side is facing up. These will be the bottom cookie of the sandwich. Scoop or pipe 1½ to 2 tablespoons of banana buttercream into the middle of the bottom cookie. Top with the remaining cookie, pressing down just so the filling spreads to the edges.

10. At room temperature, the cookies will keep fresh for 3 days; in the freezer, they will keep for 1 month.

(recipe continues)

BANANA BUTTERCREAM

Makes about 3 cups

I'm not messing around when I say "ripe banana."
I want that bad boy rrrrrripe. My go-to move: Buy
just ripening bananas a couple of days (or weeks)
before you plan to bake and toss them in an airtight
container in the freezer to age for 2 days to 2 weeks.
Thaw them, peel free, in the microwave when it's
time to bake.

→ Can't find a perfectly ripe banana? Gerber
banana baby food is an amazing substitute. It
might sound weird, but it's just a smooth puree of
perfectly ripe fruit!

→ Food coloring not your thing? I hear ya, but FYI this
frosting will not be banana yellow without it.

113g	unsalted butter, softened	1 stick (8 T)
120g	confectioners' sugar	1 cup
170g	white chocolate chips	1 cup
115g	extra-ripe banana, pureed	½ cup (about 1 banana)
45g	heavy cream	3 T
4g	vanilla extract	1 tsp
3g	kosher salt	¾ tsp
	yellow food coloring	8 drops

1. In the bowl of a stand mixer fitted with the paddle attachment, cream together the butter and confectioners' sugar on medium-high for 2 to 3 minutes. Scrape down the sides of the bowl.

2. In a microwave-safe bowl, melt the white chocolate chips in the microwave in 30-second spurts, stirring after each, until smooth. Stir the pureed banana into the melted white chocolate until completely combined. The mixture will thicken up.

3. With the mixer on low, add the white chocolate/ banana mixture and paddle to combine.

4. Still on low, add the cream, vanilla, salt, and food coloring. Increase the speed to medium and cream for 2 minutes until the buttercream is light and fluffy.

5. Transfer to a 1-gallon zip-seal bag or piping bag when ready to use.

FLUFFERNUTTERS

Makes 16 cookies · GF

In the Most Nostalgic Foods of All-Time list, the Fluffernutter is hard to beat. This school lunch box classic is texturally incredible, sure to stick to the roof of your mouth in the best way possible. Somehow, some marketing genius at Big Time Food Brand convinced mothers everywhere that a white bread sandwich of PB and marshmallow was a nutritious meal for growing children—and God bless them for it. This cookie brings the peanut butter/marshmallow marriage to the next level by eliminating the bread (and gluten!) altogether and letting the warm nuttiness get the glory. If you've never made your own marshmallows before, this is the perfect time to start—you'll be amazed at how easy it is.

→ If you're in a time crunch and need a quick sub for the homemade marshmallow, just stir 2 cups of mini marshmallows into the dough.

→ If your kitchen is particularly warm and your dough particularly sticky, chill the stuffed dough for 30 minutes to firm up.

540g	creamy peanut butter	2 cups
2	large eggs, at room temperature	
24g	vanilla extract	2 T
200g	sugar	1 cup
150g	light brown sugar	⅔ cup (packed)
8g	baking soda	2 tsp
4g	kosher salt	1 tsp
1 recipe	Vanilla Marshmallows (recipe follows)	

1. Heat the oven to 350°F. Pan-spray or line three half-sheet pans with parchment paper or silicone baking mats.

2. In the bowl of a stand mixer fitted with the paddle attachment, mix together the peanut butter, eggs, and vanilla on medium-low until smooth.

3. Add the sugar, brown sugar, baking soda, and salt and mix until just combined.

4. Using a 2-ounce cookie scoop (or a ¼-cup measure), scoop the dough onto the prepared sheet pans. Press a well in the middle of each scoop that is large enough to hold a marshmallow square. Place a marshmallow inside the dough and pinch and form the dough around it to fully encapsulate. It's okay to squish the marshmallow a bit in the process.

5. Arrange the cookies 5 to 6 per pan with at least 4 inches all around. (These cookies spread!)

6. Bake at 350°F until the edges are just dry and cracks of marshmallow are peeking through, 8 to 9 minutes. The cookies will firm up as they cool.

7. Let the cookies cool completely on the pans, then transfer to a plate or an airtight container for storage. At room temperature, the cookies will keep fresh for 3 days; in the freezer, they will keep for 1 month.

(recipe continues)

VANILLA MARSHMALLOWS

Makes sixteen ½-inch squares

→ You'll need a candy thermometer to get your marshmallow goo to just the right temperature—you can find them in most kitchen aisles.

75g	cool water	5 T, divided
6g	vanilla extract	1½ tsp
7g	unflavored gelatin	2½ tsp (1 envelope)
100g	sugar	½ cup
105g	light corn syrup	⅓ cup

1. Lightly mist an 8 × 8-inch pan with cooking spray.

2. In a stand mixer bowl, combine 45g (3 tablespoons) of the water and the vanilla. Sprinkle the gelatin evenly over the top and let sit to bloom for at least 5 minutes.

3. In a saucepan, combine the sugar, light corn syrup, and remaining 30g (2 tablespoons) water. Cook over high heat until it reaches 235°F.

4. Fit the whisk onto the stand mixer and with the mixer set to the lowest speed, quickly pour the sugar syrup into the bottom of the bowl. The heat will liquefy the gelatin mixture on contact. Once all the syrup is in the bowl, increase the speed to medium and whip for 2 minutes to cool the mixture down.

5. Increase to high speed and whip for 7 to 8 more minutes until a glossy, white, fluffy marshmallow mixture forms.

6. Lightly mist a silicone spatula with cooking spray and scrape the marshmallow into the prepared pan. Quickly spread it evenly into the corners.

7. Let the marshmallow cool for 2 hours. Use clean scissors to cut it into 16 squares. Store in an airtight container for 1 week.

LIME RITZIES

Makes about 30 sammies

In the baking professionals' universe, Mallomars aren't exactly held in high regard. Marshmallow on a plain wafer coated in regular chocolate—they aren't bringing much to the table…except a killer textural formula. These Lime Ritzies borrow from the Mallomar construction but use every component to pack in Key lime pie flavor. Swapping in a butter cracker for the base means these come together quickly. The lime in the DIY marshmallow makes these bright and full of zing. And the pineapple jam snuck into the center? I just love a good wink-wink. I would gladly welcome these to the aisle of the grocery store.

→ These are crunchiest the day they're made! They are equally delicious and every bit as lovable on days 2 and 3, but they take on an evolved, softer texture.

60	Ritz crackers	about 2 sleeves
15 T	Pineapple Jam (recipe follows)	
1 recipe	Lime Marshmallow (recipe follows)	
300g	white chocolate chips	1⅔ cups
10g	grapeseed oil	1 T
2	limes, zested	

1. Heat the oven to 350°F. Line two half-sheet pans with parchment paper or silicone baking mats.

2. Distribute the crackers across the pans and toast at 350°F until golden, 5 minutes.

3. Flip half of the crackers (30) upside down and portion a ½-tablespoon dollop of cooled pineapple jam onto the bottom of each cracker.

4. Use a piping or zip-seal bag to pipe 1 tablespoon of lime marshmallow around the edge of and above the pineapple jam, like a beehive, being careful not to pipe all the way to the edge of the cracker. You want to leave a tiny edge of cracker uncovered to avoid spillover.

5. Place a second cracker on top and press down lightly to adhere the cracker to the marshmallow and form a sandwich. Repeat with the remaining crackers.

6. In a microwave-safe bowl, melt the white chocolate chips and oil together in the microwave in 30-second spurts, stirring after each, until smooth. Make sure the white chocolate is fluid but slightly warm (not hot!) before proceeding.

7. One at a time, place a sandwich onto the tines of a fork and lower it just into the surface of the chocolate coating. Use a spoon to pour and drizzle the chocolate over the sandwich until it is completely covered.

8. Lift the coated sandwich from the chocolate coating and allow any excess to drip off. Carefully slide it back onto the remaining prepared baking pan and allow to set for 10 minutes (it's okay if a bit of chocolate pools around the bottom of the sandwich). Repeat with the entire batch.

9. Before the chocolate is completely set, use a fork or offset spatula to lift and transfer the sandwiches to a new piece of parchment, leaving any pooled chocolate behind (this is how to keep any pesky chocolate "feet" from forming around the sandwiches). Decorate the tops with a little lime zest, then allow the chocolate shell to set completely.

10. Transfer the cookies to a plate or an airtight container for storage. At room temperature, the cookies will keep fresh for 3 days; in the freezer, they will keep for 1 month.

(recipe continues)

PINEAPPLE JAM

Makes 1¼ cups (325g)

In addition to making a great filling for Lime Ritzies, this jam is great stirred into a cocktail, spooned over yogurt, or spread on buttered toast—or even a Buttered Toast Cookie (page 247).

567g	pineapple chunks	1 can (20 oz)
100g	sugar	½ cup
3g	kosher salt	¾ tsp
0.5g	ground ginger	¼ tsp
15g	lime juice	1 T

1. In a blender or food processor, puree the entire can, pineapple chunks and liquid, until smooth.

2. In a heavy-bottomed saucepan, bring the pineapple puree to a boil over high heat. Reduce the heat to medium and simmer until the liquid has mostly evaporated, about 10 minutes.

3. Reduce the heat to medium-low, add the sugar, salt, and ground ginger and cook until the pineapple turns translucent and sticky and the mixture is thickened like jam, about 10 more minutes.

4. Remove the jam from the heat and stir in the lime juice. Set aside to cool.

LIME MARSHMALLOW

Makes 1½ cups

→ You'll need a candy thermometer to get your marshmallow goo to just the right temperature—you can find them in most kitchen aisles.

→ Down to clown on even more marshmallows?! Check out the Vanilla Marshmallows (page 47) used to make marshmallow squares for the Fluffernutters (page 45).

45g	lime juice	3 T
4g	vanilla extract	1 tsp
7g	powdered gelatin	2½ tsp (1 envelope)
100g	sugar	½ cup
105g	light corn syrup	⅓ cup
30g	water	2 T
	green food coloring	4 drops

1. In a stand mixer bowl, combine the lime juice and vanilla. Sprinkle the gelatin evenly over the liquid and let sit and bloom for at least 5 minutes.

2. In a small saucepan, combine the sugar, light corn syrup, and water. Cook over high heat until it reaches 235°F.

3. Fit the whisk onto the stand mixer and, with the mixer set to the lowest speed, quickly pour the sugar syrup into the bottom of the bowl. The heat will liquefy the gelatin mixture on contact. Once all the syrup is in the bowl, increase the speed to medium and whip for 2 minutes to cool the mixture down.

4. Add the green food coloring. Increase the mixer to high speed and whip for 7 to 8 more minutes until a glossy, fluffy marshmallow mixture forms.

5. Immediately transfer the marshmallow to a piping or zip-seal bag and prepare to portion.

PLEASE MAKE SURE I AM CLOSED

6 FEET

MAINTAIN A
PHYSICAL DISTANCE

ALWAYS WEAR A MASK
IN THIS FACILITY

**MILK
BAR**

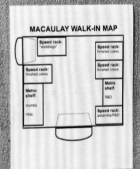

MACAULAY WALK-IN MAP

Speed rack:
"weddings"

Speed rack:
finished cakes

Speed rack:
finished cakes

Speed rack:
finished cakes

Metro
shelf:
R&D

Metro
shelf:

crumbs

misc.

Speed rack:
assembly-R&D

MACAULAY WALK-IN

TRISCUIT SANDIES

Makes 16 cookies

Adding layers of texture to a cookie by folding in ground-down bits of goodness is one of our favorite ways to pack a big punch, but you need to choose your fighter wisely. If you pick something too smooth, your cookie won't gain any oomph, and if you choose something too flavorful, your cookie may end up overwhelming (sorry, Flamin' Hot Cheetos). In search of a base that brings loads of unexpected texture and just the right amount of flavor, our journey led to woven wheat crackers. Nothing if not … textural, these pantry staples add tons of complexity, and the joy of converting something so seemingly virtuous into a cookie is just bonus points.

→ This cookie wants, nay, NEEDS Triscuits. Please don't try to sub in another cracker and expect the same results!

→ Turbinado sugar works great in this recipe because the large granules flirt with your taste buds as they bring an extra sandie moment, too. But sub in granulated sugar if needed.

190g	Triscuit crackers	38 crackers
113g	unsalted butter, softened	1 stick (8 T)
40g	confectioners' sugar	⅓ cup
110g	flour	¾ cup
15g	turbinado sugar	1 T
4g	kosher salt	1 tsp
	flour, for dusting	
25g	sugar, for sprinkling	2 T

1. Heat the oven to 325°F. Pan-spray or line one half-sheet pan with parchment paper or silicone baking mat.

2. In the bowl of a stand mixer fitted with the paddle attachment, beat the Triscuits on medium speed until the crackers are crushed into a coarse sand, about 5 minutes. Transfer to a bowl and set aside.

3. Back in the stand mixer, cream together the butter and confectioners' sugar on medium-high for 2 to 3 minutes until well combined. Scrape down the sides of the bowl.

4. Add the flour, crushed Triscuits, turbinado sugar, and salt and paddle on low speed just until the dough comes together, no longer than 1 minute. Scrape down the sides of the bowl with a spatula.

5. Scrape the dough out onto a piece of parchment paper and form into a rough square. Dust the top lightly with flour and roll into an 8 × 8-inch square. Transfer the dough to the prepared pan and freeze, uncovered, until firm, about 15 minutes.

6. Use a Triscuit to measure, score, and slice the dough into a grid of 16 Triscuit-size squares. Use the dull side of a knife blade (or the sharp side with a careful hand) to make crosshatch indentations in the cut cookies to resemble the weave of a Triscuit.

7. Bake at 325°F until golden, 14 to 16 minutes.

8. Sprinkle the tops of the warm cookies with sugar. Let cool completely on the pans, then transfer to a plate or an airtight container for storage. At room temperature, the cookies will keep fresh for 3 days; in the freezer, they will keep for 1 month.

GOOEY BUTTER COOKIES

Makes about 24 smallish cookies

If you've been around the block with me, you know my love for St. Louis gooey butter cake runs deep. Starting with my grandma's pumpkin variety, I've chased down gooey butter cake in nearly every form and flavor. Dangerously buttery and almost pudding-like, this texture reigns supreme in my eyes—I knew it deserved a place in the cookie lineup as well. It took some major baking science to get the goo level just right here while still being a cookie you can hold in your hands. Lucky for you, I've done all the tedious testing. Tough life, I know.

→ This cookie bakes high and quick. Crank up the oven, set that timer, and be nearby with oven mitts!

432g	yellow cake mix	1 box (3⅔ cups)
70g	flour	½ cup
2	large eggs	
226g	unsalted butter, melted	2 sticks (16 T)
1 recipe	Gooey Cream Cheese Filling (recipe follows)	

1. Heat the oven to 500°F and pan-spray or line two half-sheet pans with parchment paper or silicone baking mats.

2. In the bowl of a stand mixer fitted with the paddle attachment, combine the cake mix and flour and mix together on low speed for 1 minute to break up clumps.

3. Add the eggs and melted butter, increase the speed to medium-high, and beat for 2 minutes until smooth. Scrape down the sides of the bowl.

4. Freeze the dough for 10 minutes to firm up.

5. Using a ¾-ounce cookie scoop (1½ tablespoons), scoop the dough onto a clean countertop. Use your thumb to create a well, nearly all the way to the bottom, in the center of each cookie. Fill the well with 2 teaspoons of gooey cream cheese filling. Your filled cookie dough rounds should be no wider than 2½ inches across.

6. Arrange the cookies on the pans in rows of 3 cookies, columns of 4 cookies, making 12 cookies per pan.

7. Bake at 500°F for 4 to 6 minutes, watching closely, rotating the pans front to back or swapping racks halfway through, until the cookies melt and spread and begin to develop color on the edges. The intensity of a 500°F oven can vary widely, so keep a close eye to judge when the cookies look done. You want a light golden cookie, more blond than brown. They will continue to bake a bit as they cool down on the ripping-hot baking sheets!

8. Let the cookies cool completely on the pans until the filling sets fully, about 20 minutes, then transfer to a plate or an airtight container for storage. At room temperature, the cookies will keep fresh for 3 days; in the freezer, they will keep for 1 month.

GOOEY CREAM CHEESE FILLING

Makes 1 cup

226g	cream cheese, softened	8 oz
90g	confectioners' sugar	¾ cup
1	large egg yolk	
2g	vanilla extract	½ tsp

Stir all ingredients together until smooth. Freeze for 10 minutes before using.

PISTACHIO FINGERS

Makes about 24 cookies

I am a sucker for pistachio anything. It may be the Italian side of me—it's Toe-ZI for the record—or it may just be that I am drawn to color (as a full-fledged adult whose wardrobe is unapologetically 75 percent tie-dyed). These cookies take the classic Mexican wedding cookie and swap the traditional almonds or pecans for pistachios—and then up that by 100 percent for maximum nuttiness.

120g	shelled pistachios	1 cup, divided
110g	flour	¾ cup
180g	confectioners' sugar	1½ cups, divided
113g	unsalted butter, cold, cubed	1 stick (8 T)
8g	vanilla extract	2 tsp
6g	kosher salt	1½ tsp

1. Heat the oven to 350°F. Pan-spray or line two half-sheet pans with parchment paper or silicone baking mats.

2. Spread 90g (¾ cup) of the pistachios onto one of the sheet pans and toast at 350°F for 7 minutes. Cool to room temperature. Hold on to the prepared sheet pan for reuse and leave the oven on.

3. In a food processor, combine the cooled toasted pistachios and flour and pulse until the nuts are broken down completely and the mixture has darkened to the color of nut butter.

4. Add 120g (1 cup) of the confectioners' sugar, the butter cubes, vanilla, and salt and pulse until a stiff dough forms. If the processor is full, rearrange pieces of the dough as needed to evenly incorporate.

5. Portion the dough into 1-tablespoon pieces and roll into balls.

6. Sprinkle the remaining 60g (½ cup) confectioners' sugar into a small pile on your work surface and roll each dough ball through the sugar to coat. Flatten into a 1½-inch log. Arrange the cookies on the prepared pans as you roll. Press 1 pistachio into the middle of each cookie.

7. Bake at 350°F until firm to the touch and golden on the edge, 10 to 12 minutes.

8. Let the cookies cool completely on the pans. Collect the remaining pile of confectioners' sugar into a bowl for decorating.

9. Toss each cooled pistachio finger into the bowl of confectioners' sugar to coat. Use a damp finger or Q-tip to dissolve the confectioners' sugar on top of each pistachio.

10. Transfer the cookies to a plate or an airtight container for storage. At room temperature, the cookies will keep fresh for 3 days; in the freezer, they will keep for 1 month.

CHEEZ-GRITS

Makes about 100 tiny cookies

Did someone say Cheese Party?

When you're pulling long shifts in a bakery, anything salty calls out to you in a sea of sweets, hence the birth of some Milk Bar classics such as Compost Cookies (full of potato chips and pretzels) and Ritz Cracker Cookies (full of Ritz crackers; see page 127). Perhaps supreme in the salt power rankings is the Cheez-It—electric in color, satisfying in texture, and off the chain in cheez (not cheese) flavor. When I pondered the thought of what a Cheez-It cookie could be like, the rabbit hole led me to this creation: a cheese-based, crispy, savory cookie that gets its structure from corn grits (you know I love a corny moment) and is just as crushable as its orange-squared forefather.

Yes, these are the perfect guest at a cheese or charcuterie-type party, but honestly, I throw a party when I find a sandwich baggie of these in my backpack, too.

P.S. Our Culinary QA Manager, Gonxhe, turned me on to the Buffalo wing variety of Cheez-Its and I've never looked back.

→ The dough is seasoned to have a kick of heat to balance the cheese. Adjust the black and cayenne peppers up or down to achieve your desired spice level.

→ Use any corn grits you have on hand, but I find instant to be the most pleasant texturally. You can also use polenta instead, which will yield a coarser texture, or cornmeal, which will result in a finer texture.

→ This recipe yields 100 poppable cookies. If you have zilch willpower like myself, bake only half the dough and pop the rest in the freezer for when company calls.

140g	unsalted butter, softened	10 T
30g	mayonnaise	2 T
80g	sharp cheddar cheese, shredded	⅓ cup
80g	pecorino cheese, grated	1 cup
1	large egg	
0.5g	black pepper	⅛ tsp
	cayenne pepper	small pinch
180g	flour	1¼ cups
30g	instant corn grits	1 T
6g	baking powder	1½ tsp
3g	kosher salt	½ tsp

1. In a stand mixer fitted with the paddle attachment, cream together the butter, mayonnaise, cheddar, and pecorino on medium-high for 2 minutes until well combined. Scrape down the sides of the bowl with a spatula.

2. Add the egg, black pepper, and cayenne and beat until smooth.

3. Add the flour, corn grits, baking powder, and salt and paddle on low speed for 2 minutes until the dough comes together and is thoroughly combined.

4. Scoop out half the dough onto a large sheet of parchment paper and form into a rough log. Fold the paper over the log and use the flat side of a bowl scraper or a wide spatula to press along the bottom edge of the log, pressing the dough against the taut paper, to tighten and extend the log to about 11 inches. Repeat with the second half of the dough.

5. Carefully transfer the logs to a tray and refrigerate until chilled and firm, a minimum of 45 minutes. Once firm, the logs can be wrapped in foil or placed in a plastic freezer bag and frozen for up to 3 months.

6. Heat the oven to 375°F. Pan-spray or line two half-sheet pans with parchment paper or silicone baking mats.

7. Just before baking, remove 1 log from the refrigerator. Use a thin knife to slice the cookies into discs between ⅛ and ¼ inch thick, essentially as thin as you can without breaking. Don't get too caught up if an edge crumbles here or there, just press it back together. Place the sliced cookies onto the prepared pans ½ inch apart. (They don't spread much.)

8. Bake at 375°F until the edges turn golden brown, 10 to 12 minutes. Repeat with the remaining dough log.

9. Let the cookies cool slightly on the pans, then carefully transfer to a plate or an airtight container for storage. At room temperature, the cookies will keep fresh for 5 days; in the freezer, they will keep for 1 month.

BARS

AS SOMEONE WHO GETS TO CALL HERSELF A CHEF BY DAY, I LOVE A great bar cookie recipe when off duty. I don't have to pull out or power up a stand mixer, I don't have to fuss over technique, and the possibilities are just as endless as a great fudgy cookie or a gorgeous layered snap. I realized not too long ago that the baked goods I lust over most are typically in bar form. Maybe it's the 90-degree mathematician in me, or maybe it's the way a slab of a bar cookie can stay both fudgy and resolute that never ceases to amaze me.

If you're considering skipping this chapter for fear it's too pedestrian, think again. The best baked goods are the ones that sneak up on you when you least expect them. That is my thesis for the bar cookie in its finest form… and for every recipe in this chapter.

BLUEBERRY & CORN BARS

Makes 9 squares

It's no secret that I'm a SUPER corny person. Yes, I love bad dad jokes, yes, I watch bad rom-coms in my free time, and yes, anything that is corn-flavored, I've explored and devoured.

It probably runs in my family. See, one Mother's Day, my mom, always a blueberry fan, asked for a blueberry-lemon buckle. I realized it was an opportunity to come up with something she didn't even know she wanted, and really a tribute to both her and her mom, the corn matriarch of the family. So, I came up with these bars, a riff on a blueberry cobbler but with big corn cookie energy.

→ Read up on corn powder on page 14.

→ If you don't have blueberries, grab a nice jar of fruity preserves like strawberry or raspberry!

170g	unsalted butter, softened	1½ sticks (12 T)
150g	sugar	¾ cup
1	large egg yolk	
160g	flour	¾ cup + 1 T
40g	corn powder	⅓ cup
3g	kosher salt	½ tsp
1g	baking powder	¼ tsp

1 recipe Jammy Blueberries (recipe follows)

1. Heat the oven to 325°F. Pan-spray an 8 × 8-inch square baking dish.

2. In a large bowl, mix together the butter and sugar with a spatula until well combined. Mix in the egg yolk and stir until well combined, scraping down the sides of the bowl as you go. Add the flour, corn powder, salt, and baking powder and mix just until combined.

3. Spread the corny batter evenly across the surface of the greased baking dish. Spoon the jammy blueberries in large dollops on the surface of the corn mixture, intentionally leaving parts of the yellow surface bare.

4. Bake at 325°F until the edges are golden brown and the bull's-eye center is set, 45 to 50 minutes.

5. Cool completely at room temperature in the pan. Cut into 9 squares. Store in an airtight container or plastic wrapped on the counter for up to 5 days or in the fridge for up to 2 weeks.

JAMMY BLUEBERRIES

Makes 1½ cups

4.5g	flour	1½ tsp
	lemon juice	½ lemon
340g	blueberries	1¾ cup (12 oz)
50g	sugar	¼ cup
	salt	pinch

1. Place the flour in a heavy-bottomed medium pot or saucepan and stir in the lemon juice until smooth. Toss the blueberries, sugar, and salt into the saucepan with the lemon mixture to evenly coat blueberries.

2. Bring the mixture to a boil over medium-high heat, stirring intermittently. Then reduce heat to medium-low and simmer for 5 to 7 minutes until the blueberries blister, release their juices, and the mixture thickens. You should be able to pull a spatula through the mixture and leave a small peek of the pan before it fills back in.

3. Remove from heat and cool completely.

PB S'MORES BARS

Makes 9 squares

How one s'mores is a serious discussion in my family. Yes, I have already alerted Webster's that s' mores is now a verb, at least according to anyone sharing space with me from Memorial Day through Labor Day. My hub's move is to swap out the classic chocolate bar for a Reese's PB cup—pretty brilliant if you ask me. I'm the patient one at the campfire/fireplace/grill, slowly roasting my marshmallows to caramelize the exterior while turning the center into that perfect warm, consistent goo all the way through.

These bars are a love letter to these combined approaches, and perhaps one of the most requested recipes from my kitchen, even when we're planning to s' more at sunset.

→ "Graham cracker crumbs" are graham crackers you grind in a food processor or blender, but you can buy them pre-pulverized.

→ In case of a larger crowd, double this recipe and bake in a 9 × 13-inch pan, increasing the bake time to 25 to 30 minutes.

→ Big mallow person? Go for the full 2 cups on top.

Choco Bottom

42g	unsalted butter, melted	3 T
70g	sugar	⅓ cup
35g	flour	¼ cup
20g	cocoa powder	¼ cup
1g	kosher salt	¼ tsp

PB-Graham Middle

70g	unsalted butter	5 T
130g	peanut butter	½ cup
8g	vanilla extract	2 tsp
100g	sugar	½ cup
40g	graham cracker crumbs	⅓ cup
2g	kosher salt	½ tsp

Choco Marsh Top

85g	semisweet chocolate chips	½ cup
50g to 100g	mini marshmallows	1 to 2 cups, to taste

1. Heat the oven to 375°F. Pan-spray an 8 × 8-inch square baking dish.

2. **Choco Bottom:** In a medium bowl, combine the melted butter, sugar, flour, cocoa powder, and salt and stir with a spatula to combine. Pour the mixture into the greased baking dish. Using your palm and fingertips, firmly and evenly press the mixture until it covers the dish's bottom evenly.

3. **PB-Graham Middle:** In a clean microwave-safe medium bowl, melt the butter in the microwave in 10-second spurts until it's liquid. Add the peanut butter and vanilla and mix with a spatula until smooth. Stir in the sugar, graham cracker crumbs, and salt until combined. Pour the peanut butter/graham cracker mixture over the chocolate base, spreading evenly to cover the bottom layer entirely.

4. **Choco Marsh Top:** Sprinkle the chocolate chips and marshmallows on top of the graham layer.

5. Bake at 375°F until your kitchen smells like a PB paradise and your marshmallows have begun to puff and take on a caramelized color, about 20 minutes.

6. If you want a little more of a campfire vibe for your creation, turn on the broiler and broil the topping until toasted to your preference, 30 to 60 seconds.

7. Cool completely before cutting into 9 squares. Store in an airtight container or plastic wrapped at room temperature for up to 5 days or in the fridge for up to 2 weeks.

MILK BAR PIE BARS

Makes 9 squares

Ask anyone on my team my top two questions when we're tasting a potential new creation for the bakery, and they will tell you they are:

1. Think it could be a little sweeter?
2. Can you give it more goo?

It's no surprise that this dense, sweet, gooey monster is a deep part of Milk Bar's flavor and textural heritage and is also the one that best represents what excites me about this world. I love that its look is unassuming and its composition impossible to wrap your head around—two of my favorite qualities in an excellent human and a baked good.

This bar is my go-to recipe when I don't feel like going to pie town. It turns the classic Milk Bar Pie ratio upside down: This is about 2 parts toasted oat cookie crust to 1 part gooey, buttery filling. And no one's mad at it.

→ Read more on corn powder, page 14. If you don't have freeze-dried corn (and therefore can't make corn powder), substitute with corn flour, all-purpose flour, or anything flavorful you can grind down (pretzel powder is usually my stand-in). It's not exactly the same, but likely only you will know the difference.

→ Read more on milk powder, page 17. I don't recommend making this recipe without it—it adds a depth and chew that is essential!

Toasted Oat Crust

56g	unsalted butter, softened	4 T
35g	light brown sugar	3 T
18g	sugar	1½ T
1	large egg	
60g	rolled oats	¾ cup
35g	flour	¼ cup
2g	kosher salt	½ tsp
0.25g	baking powder	a pinch

Gooey Butter Filling

200g	sugar	1 cup
110g	light brown sugar	½ cup (packed)
16g	milk powder	2 T
1.25g	corn powder	1 tsp
2g	kosher salt	½ tsp
170g	unsalted butter, melted	1½ sticks (12 T)
4g	vanilla extract	1 tsp
6	large egg yolks	

Confectioners' sugar, to finish

1. Heat the oven to 350°F. Pan-spray an 8 × 8-inch square baking dish.

2. **Toasted Oat Crust:** In a large bowl, mix together the butter, brown sugar, and sugar with a spatula until well combined. Mix in the egg and stir until well combined, scraping down the sides of the bowl as you go. Add the oats, flour, salt, and baking powder, and mix just until combined. Pour this mixture into the greased baking dish and use a spatula to evenly spread the mixture, fully covering the dish's bottom.

(recipe continues)

3. Bake at 350°F until the edges of the crust are golden brown, about 20 minutes. Cool at room temperature for 10 minutes. Leave the oven on.

4. **Gooey Butter Filling:** In a large bowl, whisk together the sugar, brown sugar, milk powder, corn powder, and salt. Whisk in the melted butter, vanilla, and egg yolks and stir until smooth. Try not to aerate the batter; mix slowly and gently. Pour this mixture on top of the oat crust, spreading evenly to all sides of the baking dish, covering the bottom layer entirely.

5. Bake at 350°F until the top and edges are golden brown and the bull's-eye center is still a bit jiggly, about 20 minutes. While baking, make room in your freezer for this baking dish.

6. Remove from the oven and ideally transfer the pan to an empty freezer to cool completely. This not only cools down the greatest bite you might ever bake, but also ensures that all the steam pockets subside. The result is a dense and gooey bar cookie, which is also much easier to portion when frozen.

7. Cut into 9 squares. Dust with confectioners' sugar before serving, if desired. Store in an airtight container or plastic wrapped on the counter for up to 5 days or in the fridge for up to 2 weeks. Feel free to hide these in the freezer, no one will go looking for them there (wink).

CASHEW PRALINE BLONDIES

Makes 9 squares

I'm pretty sure I used to chant "Bring on the brownies" in my sleep. I loved melting down chocolate chips and stirring them into basic ingredients to yield this wonderfully dense and fudgy creation, always with something new and fun I'd swirl into the top before baking.

When I finally discovered the vanilla version of the chocolate brownie, I started tinkering with the recipe. Most blondie recipes don't have chocolate in them, but adding a small amount of white chocolate gives them the same density and texture of a luscious brownie.

Because blondies read a bit sweeter than their semisweet chocolate cousins, I swear by this quick cashew praline swirl-in. It brings a nutty, toffee counterbalance of flavor and killer pop of microscopic texture from little shards of brittle—entirely unassuming, then POW! A total knockout.

Cashew Praline

70g	sugar	⅓ cup
48g	unsalted roasted cashews	⅓ cup
1g	kosher salt	¼ tsp
25g	vegetable oil	1 T + 2 tsp

Blondie Base

113g	unsalted butter	1 stick (8 T)
60g	white chocolate chips	⅓ cup
100g	sugar	½ cup
110g	light brown sugar	½ cup (packed)
1	large egg	
4g	vanilla extract	1 tsp
115g	flour	¾ cup + 1 T
4g	kosher salt	1 tsp

1. **Cashew Praline:** Pan-spray a half-sheet pan. Make a dry caramel: In a heavy-bottomed medium saucepan, cook the sugar over medium-high heat. As soon as the sugar starts to melt, use a heat-resistant spatula to move it constantly around the pan—you want it all to melt and caramelize evenly to a gorgeous amber color. Remove the pan from the heat and with a heat-resistant spatula, stir in the cashews, making sure all are coated in caramel. Then swiftly dump the contents of the pan out onto the prepared half-sheet pan, spreading it as thin and even as possible. Let the brittle cool completely.

2. Once cool, with a meat pounder or heavy rolling pin, break the brittle up into small pieces. Transfer the brittle to a food processor, add the salt and oil, and grind down until it has nearly liquefied but still has little shards of brittle.

3. Heat the oven to 325°F. Pan-spray an 8 × 8-inch square baking dish.

4. **Blondie Base:** In a large microwave-safe bowl, melt the butter and white chocolate chips in the microwave in 30-second spurts, stirring after each, until smooth. Mix in the sugar and brown sugar. Mix in the egg and vanilla and stir until well combined, scraping down the sides of the bowl as you go. Add the flour and salt, and mix just until combined.

(recipe continues)

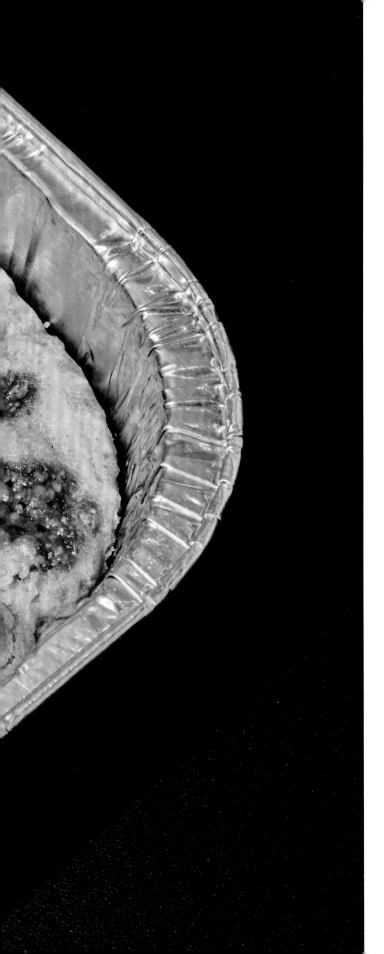

5. Spread the blondie batter evenly across the surface of the greased baking dish. Spoon the cashew praline in large dollops on the surface of the blondie mixture, then, with the tip of a butter knife, swirl the batter and praline into each other, leaving peeks and pops of both.

6. Bake at 325°F until the edges are golden brown and the bull's-eye center is set, 40 to 45 minutes.

7. Cool completely in the pan. Cut into 9 squares. Store in an airtight container or plastic wrapped on the counter for up to 5 days or in the fridge for up to 2 weeks.

PUMPKIN DULCE BARS

Makes 9 squares

I fell in love with the combo of pumpkin and dulce de leche (sweetened condensed milk cooked down to a caramelized state) when we dreamed it up as the star layers of a cinnamon-butterscotch sponge cake at Milk Bar. When I need to get a quick fix of this killer combo, I turn to these simple yet marvelous bars, both crumble-textured and smooth.

→ You can ABSOLUTELY make your own dulce de leche! Read more on page 14. But no shade if you buy it either.

→ Because there's cream cheese in these babies, you want to store them in the fridge only!

Cinnamon Crust

115g	flour	⅔ cup + 2 T
50g	sugar	¼ cup
1g	ground cinnamon	½ tsp
2g	kosher salt	½ tsp
85g	unsalted butter, melted	6 T

Dulce de Leche Layer

175g	dulce de leche	⅔ cup

Pumpkin Layer

75g	cream cheese	6 oz
100g	sugar	½ cup
1g	kosher salt	¼ tsp
0.5g	ground cinnamon	⅛ tsp
1	large egg	
75g	unsweetened canned pumpkin puree	⅓ cup
4g	vanilla extract	1 tsp

1. Heat the oven to 350°F. Pan-spray an 8 × 8-inch square baking dish.

2. **Cinnamon Crust:** In a large bowl, mix together the flour, sugar, cinnamon, and salt with a spatula until well combined. Mix in the melted butter and toss to combine. Transfer the mixture to the greased baking dish. Using your palm and fingertips, firmly and evenly press it in, covering the dish's bottom.

3. **Dulce de Leche Layer:** Pour all of the dulce de leche on top of the crust, spreading evenly to cover the bottom layer entirely.

4. **Pumpkin Layer:** In a large bowl, stir together the cream cheese, sugar, salt, and cinnamon until smooth. Stir in the egg, pumpkin, and vanilla and mix until smooth and well combined. Pour this mixture atop the dulce de leche, spreading evenly to all sides of the baking dish, covering the dulce layer entirely.

5. Bake at 350°F until the pumpkin top is set but still jiggles back at you, 40 to 45 minutes.

6. Cool completely in the pan. Cut into 9 squares. Store in an airtight container or plastic wrapped in the fridge for up to 2 weeks.

PERFECT 10 BARS

Makes 9 squares · V · GF

Call it old age, but lately I've really been jamming on chewy granola bars. The deep nuttiness, the toothsome oats, the pops of sweetness and acidity from the chocolate chips, the twinkle of salt at the end. I just can't get enough. So in R&D land for this book, I set out to nail a chewy granola bar. When I did, I realized the recipe was a cross between a mix of the grocery store, brown-paper-bag lunch classic and the Perfect 10 Kookie, an insanely delicious gluten-free, dairy-free almond-oatmeal-chocolate chip cookie of sorts my sweet friend Karlie Kloss and I made to raise money for school lunches nationwide (more than $1 million!). It's a be-good, do-good kind of spirit that surrounds these ingredients.

→ If you're truly gluten-free, check that those oats meet the GF mark, and if you're vegan, check that you're using dairy-free chocolate chips.

→ Make sure to use old-fashioned rolled oats, not quick oats or steel-cut oats.

→ Feel free to substitute any nuts for the pecans and any nut butter (or peanut butter) for the almond butter; those are just my favorites.

→ Jonesing for more? This recipe is easy to double and bake in a 9 × 13-inch baking dish for 55 to 60 minutes.

140g	maple syrup	½ cup
75g	olive oil	¼ cup + 1 T
70g	almond butter	3 T
12g	vanilla extract	1 T
80g	rolled oats	1 cup
45g	almond flour	½ cup
7g	cornstarch	1 T
6g	kosher salt	1½ tsp
55g	pecans, toasted and chopped	½ cup
60g	chocolate chips	⅓ cup

1. Heat the oven to 325°F. Pan-spray an 8 × 8-inch square baking dish.

2. In a large bowl, mix together the maple syrup, olive oil, almond butter, and vanilla with a whisk until well combined. Add the oats, almond flour, cornstarch, and salt and mix to combine with a spatula. Stir in the pecans and chocolate chips. Transfer the mixture to the greased baking dish, spreading evenly to all sides, covering the bottom entirely.

3. Bake at 325°F until the bars are a deep, gooey golden brown all around, about 45 minutes.

4. Cool completely in the pan. Cut into 9 squares. Store in an airtight container or plastic wrapped on the counter for up to 5 days or in the fridge for up to 2 weeks.

STRAWBERRY-PRETZEL ICE CREAM BARS

Makes 18 bars

The combination of sweet strawberry jam and salty mini pretzels has been a life hack of mine since I started raiding the pantry for curious snacks as a kid. In 2007, when I was finding my voice creating plated desserts at Momofuku, I knew I wanted to find a way to celebrate this killer combo. I experimented with jam, crumble, crunch, ganache, ice cream, fudge—the flavor duo has slayed through all forms. But my favorite way to bring this combo to life in shareable form at home? These bars. They're different, yet simple, and fully crushable year-round.

→ If you're not the pretzel type, substitute 40g Ritz crackers (1 cup/13 crackers).

→ If you're not the strawberry type but are curious about the fruit-pretzel combo, sub in 1 pint of raspberries.

→ In case of a larger crowd, double this recipe and bake in a 9 × 13-inch pan, increasing the bake time to 25 to 30 minutes.

Pretzel Crust

25g	mini pretzels	¾ cup
50g	flour	⅓ cup
25g	sugar	2 T
22g	light brown sugar	1½ T
1g	baking powder	¼ tsp
1g	baking soda	¼ tsp
0.5g	kosher salt	⅛ tsp
20g	grapeseed oil	2 T
85g	white chocolate chips	½ cup

Strawberry No-Churn Ice Cream

453g	strawberries, hulled	1 lb
25g	sugar	2 T
220g	heavy cream	1 cup
396g	sweetened condensed milk	1 can (14 oz)
2g	kosher salt	½ tsp

1. Heat the oven to 300°F. Pan-spray a half-sheet pan and an 8 × 8-inch square baking dish.

2. **Pretzel Crust:** Blitz the pretzels in a blender until they are a fine powder. In a large bowl, combine 2 tablespoons of the pretzel powder, the flour, sugar, brown sugar, baking powder, baking soda, and salt. Add the oil and use your hands or a spatula to mix everything until you have clumpy crumbs. Spread the crumbs out evenly on the half-sheet pan.

3. Bake at 300°F until the pretzel crumbs are ever-so-slightly dried out and caramelized, 15 to 20 minutes. Let the pretzel crumbs cool completely.

4. In a microwave-safe bowl, melt the white chocolate chips in the microwave in 30-second spurts, stirring after each, until smooth. Toss in the remaining 2 tablespoons pretzel powder and the cooled pretzel crumbs and stir to coat in the white chocolate.

5. Transfer the pretzel crust mixture to the greased baking dish. Using your palm and fingertips, firmly and evenly press it in, fully covering the dish's bottom.

6. **Strawberry No-Churn Ice Cream:** In a food processor or blender, puree the strawberries and sugar until entirely liquid.

7. In a large bowl, whip the heavy cream to medium peaks. Whisk in the sweetened condensed milk and salt. Whisk in the strawberry puree until the cream has an even, light pink hue. Pour this mixture atop the pretzel crust, spreading evenly to cover the pretzel layer entirely.

8. Freeze until the ice cream is firm to the touch, a minimum of 6 hours.

9. Cut into 9 squares. Then cut each square in half to make a rectangle. Store in the freezer in an airtight container or plastic wrapped for up to 1 month.

CARAMEL APPLE-WALNUT BARS

Makes 18 bars

There is a bakery in Cambridge, Massachusetts, called Sofra. They make these caramel cashew bars that are to LIVE for. Whenever anyone I know is anywhere in the vicinity of Boston, I beg them to visit the incredible baker, Maura Kilpatrick, and bring me home a box (or four) of her creation. However much they bring me, it's never enough, so I set out to find my own way to a Tosi version of the Kilpatrick classic. This is something I can make at home, subbing in any juice and nut for the apple juice and walnut, respectively. On a dense, buttery shortbread crust, you really can't go wrong with any choice. This is my go-to when the fall feels hit and I find myself wrapped in plaid and flannel.

→ These bars set after they come out of the oven. Many of you will be tempted to leave them in the oven longer, but that will destroy the caramel's texture once cooled. Trust me on the short baking time!

Shortbread Crust

160g	flour	1 cup + 2 T
40g	light brown sugar	3 T
1g	kosher salt	¼ tsp
84g	unsalted butter, melted	6 T

Caramel Apple Layer

200g	sugar	1 cup
110g	light brown sugar	½ cup (packed)
62g	apple juice	¼ cup
30g	heavy cream	2 T
56g	unsalted butter	4 T
2g	kosher salt	½ tsp
210g	walnut halves	2 cups

1. Heat the oven to 350°F. Pan-spray an 8 × 8-inch square baking dish.

2. **Shortbread Crust:** In a large bowl, mix together the flour, brown sugar, and salt with a spatula until well combined. Mix in the melted butter and toss to combine. Transfer the mixture to the greased baking dish. Using your palm and fingertips, firmly and evenly press it in, fully covering the dish's bottom.

3. Bake at 350°F until the crust is a light golden brown, about 15 minutes. Set aside to cool. Leave the oven on.

4. **Caramel Apple Layer:** Make a dry caramel: In a heavy-bottomed medium saucepan, cook 50g (¼ cup) of the sugar over medium-high heat. As soon as the sugar starts to melt, use a heat-resistant spatula to move it constantly around the pan—you want it all to melt and caramelize evenly to a gorgeous amber color. Add an additional 50g (¼ cup) of the sugar to the existing caramel in the pan, repeating the previous steps—cook and stir, cook and stir, until the mixture is once again a gorgeous amber color. Continue adding 50g (¼ cup) of the sugar twice more until all your sugar has become one pretty pan of caramel. Stir in the brown sugar, mixing just until it dissolves.

5. Remove the saucepan from the heat. Very slowly and very carefully, stir in the apple juice and heavy cream. The caramel will bubble up and steam; stand away until the steam dissipates. Use a heat-resistant spatula to stir the mixture together. Then add the butter and salt, stirring continuously. If the mixture is at all lumpy, put the saucepan back over medium heat and cook, stirring constantly, until the sugar bits have dissolved and the mixture is smooth.

6. Stir in the walnuts, mixing carefully to coat them entirely. Let the caramel cool to room temperature.

7. Pour the caramel apple/walnut mixture onto the crust, spreading evenly to cover the bottom layer entirely.

8. Bake at 350°F until the nuts have toasted deeply, about 15 minutes.

9. Cool completely in the pan. Cut into 9 squares. Then cut each square on the diagonal to make 18 triangles. Store in an airtight container or plastic wrapped on the counter for up to 5 days or in the fridge for up to 2 weeks.

GRASSHOPPER PIE BARS

Makes 9 bars

For a long time, I didn't fancy myself a mint and chocolate aficionado. I would turn my nose up at Junior Mints, After Eights (though we can all agree it's a great name), and York Peppermint Patties. That is, until we decided to put Grasshopper Pie on the menu during our first holiday season at Milk Bar—essentially a fudgy brownie set in a graham cracker crust with layers of mint cheesecake and a mint glaze. I became a convert in a big way! This is my translation of it in bar cookie form, perfect before or after 8 p.m.

→ Peppermint extract is not the same as mint extract. Mint extract has more of a spearmint or toothpaste-type flavor. Even though it won't really feel like you're brushing your teeth if you can only get your hands on mint extract, I highly recommend sourcing peppermint extract!

Brownie Base

113g	unsalted butter	1 stick (8 T)
85g	chocolate chips	½ cup
200g	sugar	1 cup
2	large eggs	
6g	vanilla extract	1½ tsp
70g	flour	½ cup
25g	cocoa powder	¼ cup
2g	kosher salt	½ tsp

Mint Cheesecake Swirl

40g	white chocolate chips	¼ cup
20g	vegetable oil	1 T + 1 tsp
55g	cream cheese	2 oz
2g	peppermint extract	½ tsp
	green food coloring	1 to 2 drops
12g	confectioners' sugar	1 T + 1 tsp
0.5g	kosher salt	⅛ tsp

Grasshopper Drizzle

60g	white chocolate chips	⅓ cup
5g	vegetable oil	1 tsp
	peppermint extract	2 drops
	green food coloring	1 drop

1. Heat the oven to 350°F. Pan-spray an 8 × 8-inch square baking dish.

2. **Brownie Base:** In a large microwave-safe bowl, melt the butter and chocolate chips together in 30-second spurts, stirring after each, until smooth. Mix in the sugar, eggs, and vanilla and stir until well combined, scraping down the sides of the bowl as you go. Add the flour, cocoa powder, and salt and mix just until combined. Transfer to the greased baking dish and spread the brownie base evenly, covering the bottom entirely.

3. **Mint Cheesecake Swirl:** In a small microwave-safe bowl, heat the white chocolate chips and oil together in 15-second spurts, stirring after each, until melted and smooth. Mix in the cream cheese, peppermint extract, and green food coloring. Pop the bowl back in the microwave for a 15-second spurt if the mixture seizes up. Mix in the confectioners' sugar and salt, and stir until smooth.

4. Spoon the mint cheesecake swirl in large dollops on the surface of the brownie base, then with the tip of a butter knife, swirl the two together, leaving peeks and pops of both.

5. Bake at 350°F until the bull's-eye center is set but the mint cheesecake has not taken on too much color, about 30 minutes. Cool completely at room temperature in the pan.

6. **Grasshopper Drizzle:** In a small microwave-safe bowl, heat the white chocolate chips and oil in the microwave in 15-second spurts, stirring after each, until melted and smooth. Mix in the

peppermint extract and food coloring to combine. Dunk the tines of a fork into the warm drizzle, then dangle the fork about 1 inch above the baking dish, channeling your inner Jackson Pollock.

7. Pop the dish into the fridge for the mint glaze to firm up—10 to 15 minutes. Cut into 9 squares. Store in an airtight container or plastic wrapped on the counter for up to 5 days or in the fridge for up to 2 weeks.

PARTY BARS

Makes 18 bars

Whenever a friend is planning to come visit for the weekend, I ask them what they request for dessert for our slumber party. If they don't have an answer, I ask them to name their favorite cookie, their favorite salty/cracker bit, their favorite nutty snack, and their favorite melty thing.

So, I have this friend named Kevin. And every time he's planning a visit, I grab the phone from my husband, and before I even ask, he shouts the same four things: Graham crackers! Ritz crackers! Coconut! Butterscotch! Also, every time Kevin comes to visit, it's an absolute party. So these bars are named in honor of him.

→ Substitute any cookie, cracker, nutty thing, or melty element for the graham, Ritz, coconut, and butterscotch, respectively. The sweetened condensed milk is essentially the glue that bonds them all together like dessert magic.

→ In case of a larger crowd, double this recipe and bake in a 9 × 13-inch pan, increasing the bake time to 30 to 35 minutes.

Graham Crust

80g	graham cracker crumbs	⅔ cup (5 crackers ground down)
56g	unsalted butter, melted	4 T

Party Layers

75g	sweetened shredded coconut	¾ cup
170g	butterscotch chips	¾ cup
85g	Ritz crackers, lightly crushed	1¾ cups (26 crackers)
375g	sweetened condensed milk	1¼ cups

1. Heat the oven to 375°F. Pan-spray an 8 × 8-inch square baking dish.

2. **Graham Crust:** In a large bowl, mix together the graham cracker crumbs and melted butter with a spatula until well combined. Transfer the graham crust mixture to the greased baking dish. Using your palm and fingertips, firmly and evenly press it in, fully covering the dish's bottom.

3. **Party Layers:** Scatter each party layer down—first the shredded coconut atop the pressed graham crust, then the butterscotch chips, and then the Ritz crackers. Pour the sweetened condensed milk into a spouted measuring cup and then drizzle over the Ritz, zigging and zagging back and forth, covering the entire surface. The sweetened condensed milk will spread evenly on its own once it hits the heat of the oven, so don't stress too much.

4. Bake at 375°F until the crackers have toasted slightly and the sweetened condensed milk has started to caramelize, 20 to 25 minutes.

5. Cool completely in the pan. Cut into 9 squares. Then cut each square in half to make 18 rectangles. Store in an airtight container or plastic wrapped on the counter for up to 5 days or in the fridge for up to 2 weeks.

THE MILK BAR COOKIE SWAP

AFTER THIRTEEN YEARS OF BUSINESS, MILK BAR HAS developed a few traditions. Team birthdays are met with custom cake creations. Every March we have our "December" holiday costume party—ah, the joys of working in the hospitality industry. And just before Thanksgiving, we have a family meal fit for royalty. But the most magical might just be the annual cookie swap.

Like most good traditions, the cookie swap was not so much designed but born out of the hilarity of life. During our first winter season as a bakery, I looked up one day from my cookie-scooping battle station and realized that the holidays were approaching at breakneck speed, and we had hardly enough time to sleep, let alone shop for gifts for loved ones. While we get plenty of joy in baking for our customers, it didn't seem right that the season would pass us by without a chance to share that feeling with our own families. I hatched a plan.

I ordered boxes of blank cookie tins and asked the team how they felt about baking a single batch of cookies in their "free time"—whatever kind they wanted!—for an old-fashioned cookie swap. They were in, and the first annual Milk Bar cookie swap was on: December 22, 2008.

I knew the team would show up big—bakers gonna bake, you know?— but what blew me away and still humbles me to this day is the glimpse we got into the individual cookie minds I spent all my waking time with. That I could work side by side with someone for months on end and still be completely surprised by the cookie they dreamt up and proudly shared. When the clock struck 1 p.m. (family meal time for Milk Bar insiders), we set up the stash of cookie tins at one end and lined up every drop cookie, bar cookie, crinkle cookie, piped creation, and gingerbread-man-holding-a-mini-cornflake-marshmallow-cookie side by side and walked the line, oohing and aaahing as we carefully filled our individual tins, the most brilliant stash that we'd each gift the family that would host us for the holiday.

We do this cookie swap to this day. Milk Bar attracts hardbodies from every corner of life, and our cookie swap table has become the most beautiful representation of just how wonderfully unique our team is. We're a group of bakers who have made the same recipe, by the tens of thousands, day in and day out, and no two cookies at the swap are ever the same.

As our fam has grown to new cities and welcomed in loads of new folks to the fold, including not only more bakers but also financial analysts, operations gurus, bakery teammates, digital experience legends, marketing pros, and talent supporters, the Milk Bar cookie swap continues to be this awe-inspiring moment that reminds me that we are more than the sum of our parts, we are a company of individuals who all bring their own cookie to the tin.

Jimbo "Peek-A-Boo!"

Potato Chip Shorties

Peach S

Chocolate Confetti

RITZ

Cornflake Choc Chip
Marshmallow

DENSE & FUDGIES

Marbled
Chocolate
S'more
Cookies
110

Peachy
Shortcake
Cookies
113

Ritz
Cracker
Cookies
127

Cocoa
Mint Chip
Cookies
99

Little
Motivators
103

Sugar Sugar Cookies
104

Cheesecake
Cookies
106

CTC Marsh
Cookies
115

Cinnamon Bun
Cookies
124

Butterscotch Pecan
Pudding Cookies
109

Chipless
Wonders
128

Nana
Nillas
135

Strawberry
Shortcake
Cookies
121

Cherry Pie
Cookies
118

Chocolate
Malted Brownie
Cookies
132

French
Toast
Cookies
136

Dulce de
Leche
Cookies
100

Carrot
Cake
Cookies
139

Pretzel
Chocolate
Chunk Cookies
122

Cereal Milk Cream
Soda Cookies
96

LONG BEFORE I MASTERED THE ART OF THE FRIENDSHIP BRACELET

or earned my keep mowing the lawn, I knew the superpowers of a dense and fudgy cookie. You know, the ones with the soft, dreamy centers. They're by far my favorite dough to snack on, my favorite cookies to pack in baggies or stack high on a plate to sprinkle out in the world.

Back then, it was the only style of cookie I knew how to make. But even as I've grown as a baker, that simple soft-centered cookie has always been the canvas on which I most love to create, the lens through which I see every flavor story come together first.

I have a theory: If I can bring a flavor story to life through a dense and fudgy cookie, it can go on to become any and every form of dessert. I can never stop thinking about how the simplicity of this basic cookie can lead to precise balancing acts of flavor and texture.

So, come along as I share some of my favorites from the past and some of the cookies I'm most excited about now. And most of all, I hope that as you read, you find ways to bake up your own creations!

It's simple. Reach out and grab inspiration—or let it sneak up on you. Then test your idea out by weaving it through the dense and fudgy cookie form.

What flavor should the base dough be? Deep vanilla? Corn? Strawberry? Is it more than one flavor of dough? A pinch and twist like the Cinnamon Bun Cookies (page 124)?

How do the other elements of the flavor story come into play? Do you want to use mix-ins like baking chips or your own Cinnamon Chips (page 117), Pie Crumbs (page 119), Cornflake Crunch (page 159), or something equally unexpected, like a sprinkling of instant espresso or a sleeve of Ritz crackers?

Is the cookie more base dough or more mix-ins? Do you stuff the dough? Do you roll the dough in something? Do you want to paint it with a glaze and sprinkles? Do you scoop them big or small? Do you spike up the baking temperature for outer caramelization or do you bake them a little lower for a greater spread? I could go on, but if you're anything like me, your mouth is watering, your imagination is firing in every direction, and your feet are tapping the ground like you're running in place. So let's GO!

CEREAL MILK CREAM SODA COOKIES

Makes 12 to 18 cookies

It was more than a decade ago that I created my first dessert based on cereal milk. It was a panna cotta, inspired by the offerings of my favorite 24/7 bodega (that's what neighborhood convenience stores are called in NYC). I had no idea I was hitting on a nostalgic pulse point for so many people. I only knew that growing up, the only way my saint of a mother could get me to drink my milk was by bribing me with sweet cereal to accompany it. In the years since it first hit the Momofuku menu, cereal milk as a flavor has been replicated in just about every form under the sun, found all over grocery store aisles. (No hard feelings! Cereal milk for everyone!) But trying to re-create the flavor in a cookie on its own was bland. I found it needed a little more to stick the landing, so I re-imagined it here with my childhood indulgence, cream soda. I never had the opportunity to pour a bottle of that good stuff over my cereal while Mom wasn't looking, but I can certainly vouch for the flavor combo in cookie form.

→ Clear vanilla extract is key to the dreamy note of the classic soda. Read more on page 15.

→ If you've ever made my cereal milk from past cookbooks, you know the deal with freeze-dried corn and corn powder made from freeze-dried corn. If you need a little guidance, read more on page 14.

→ The sodium citrate and citric acid bring the cream soda flavors to life; otherwise, it's a flat vanilla flavor. They're essential in this cookie. But remember, a little goes a long way. Read more on page 14.

80g	Frosted Flakes	2½ cups
226g	unsalted butter, softened	2 sticks (16 T)
125g	sugar	½ cup + 2 T
170g	dark brown sugar	¾ cup (packed)
1	large egg	
8g	clear vanilla extract	2 tsp
270g	flour	2 cups
12g	milk powder	2 T
7.5g	corn powder	2 T
6g	kosher salt	1½ tsp
3g	baking soda	½ tsp
2g	baking powder	½ tsp
2g	citric acid	½ tsp
1g	sodium citrate	¼ tsp
125g	white chocolate chips	¾ cup
100g	mini marshmallows	2 cups

1. Heat the oven to 300°F.

2. Spread the Frosted Flakes onto a baking sheet and toast in the oven until fragrant, about 10 minutes. Cool completely.

3. Increase the oven temperature to 350°F. Pan-spray or line two half-sheet pans with parchment paper or silicone baking mats.

4. In the bowl of a stand mixer fitted with the paddle attachment, cream together the butter, sugar, and brown sugar on medium-high for 4 minutes until well combined. Scrape down the sides of the bowl, add the egg and vanilla, and mix for 4 more minutes.

5. Add the flour, milk powder, corn powder, salt, baking soda, baking powder, citric acid, and sodium citrate and paddle on low speed until just combined, about 20 seconds.

6. Paddle in the white chocolate chips, cooled Frosted Flakes, and mini marshmallows until just incorporated.

7. Using a 2¾-ounce cookie scoop (or a ⅓-cup measure), scoop the dough onto the prepared pans 2 to 3 inches apart.

8. Bake at 350°F until golden around the edges, 8 to 10 minutes.

9. Cool completely on the pans before serving. Transfer the cookies to a plate or an airtight container for storage. At room temperature, the cookies will keep fresh for 3 days; in the freezer, they will keep for 1 month.

COCOA MINT CHIP COOKIES

Makes 12 to 18 cookies

In the endless world of flavor combinations, there are some tried-and-true duos that deliver time after time. Chocolate and peanut butter. Vanilla and sprinkles. Cinnamon and butterscotch. But there is something really, really special about fudgy cocoa and crisp, breezy mint. Together, the two flavors elevate each other until you are left with a supremely satisfying cookie that hits you smack-dab in the after-dinner-mint-memory sweet spot, making these the perfect cookies to eat in your PJs just before hitting the lights.

300g	sugar	1½ cups
226g	unsalted butter, softened	2 sticks (16 T)
1	large egg	
4g	peppermint extract	1 tsp
315g	semisweet chocolate chips	1¾ cups, divided
145g	flour	1 cup
65g	cocoa powder	¾ cup
6g	salt	1½ tsp
4g	baking powder	1 tsp
3g	baking soda	½ tsp
255g	mint baking chips	1½ cups

1. Heat the oven to 350°F. Pan-spray or line two half-sheet pans with parchment paper or silicone baking mats.

2. In the bowl of a stand mixer fitted with the paddle attachment, cream together the sugar and butter on medium-high for 4 minutes until well combined. Scrape down the sides of the bowl, add the egg and peppermint extract, and mix for 4 more minutes.

3. In a microwave-safe bowl, melt 60g (¼ cup) of the chocolate chips in the microwave in 30-second spurts, stirring after each, until smooth. Add this to the mixer bowl and mix to combine.

4. Add the flour, cocoa powder, salt, baking powder, and baking soda and paddle on low speed until just combined, about 20 seconds.

5. Paddle in the remaining 255g (1½ cups) chocolate chips and the mint chips, just until incorporated.

6. Using a 2¾-ounce cookie scoop (or a ⅓-cup measure), scoop the dough onto the prepared pans 2 to 3 inches apart. Flatten the domed tops with your palm (it will be a bit sticky, don't worry).

7. Bake at 350°F until crispy around the edges, 8 to 10 minutes.

8. Let the cookies cool briefly on the pans, then transfer to a plate or an airtight container for storage. At room temperature, the cookies will keep fresh for 3 days; in the freezer, they will keep for 1 month.

DULCE DE LECHE COOKIES

Makes 12 cookies

As a lover of science and a baking dork to my core, the idea of caramel always excites me. How cool is it that sugar, with nothing more than a bit of heat and some patience, can transform completely into a rich, flavorful goo? I have had to learn to restrain myself from adding caramel to recipes—while it's delicious, it's not always necessary. But this? This cookie is really just a vessel to get more caramel—or in this case, canned dulce de leche (a creamy Latin American milk-based caramel you can find at most grocery stores)—into my life, letting the gooey warm flavor be the star of the show.

→ You can ABSOLUTELY make your own dulce de leche! Read more on page 14. But no shade if you buy it either.

140g	unsalted butter, softened	10 T
380g	dulce de leche	1 cup, divided
250g	sugar	1¼ cups
1	large egg	
4g	vanilla extract	1 tsp
250g	flour	1¾ cups
6g	kosher salt	1½ tsp
2g	baking powder	½ tsp
1.5g	baking soda	¼ tsp
120g	confectioners' sugar	1 cup

1. Heat the oven to 350°F. Pan-spray or line two half-sheet pans with parchment paper or silicone baking mats.

2. In the bowl of a stand mixer fitted with the paddle attachment, cream together the butter, 95g (¼ cup) of the dulce de leche, and the sugar on medium-high for 2 to 3 minutes until well combined. Scrape down the sides of the bowl, add the egg and vanilla, and mix for 2 more minutes.

3. Add the flour, salt, baking powder, and baking soda and paddle on low speed until just combined, about 20 seconds.

4. Fill a 2¾-ounce cookie scoop (or a ⅓-cup measure) most of the way with dough. Scoop into the palm of your hand. With your thumb, create a well in the center. Fill the well with 1 tablespoon of the remaining dulce de leche, seal the edges of the dough with your finger, and roll into a ball. Repeat with the remaining dough.

5. Roll each ball in a bowl of confectioners' sugar and arrange on the sheet pans 2 to 3 inches apart. Use the palm of your hand to gently flatten the domes of dough slightly.

6. Bake at 350°F until lightly brown on the edges, 10 to 12 minutes.

7. Let the cookies cool briefly on the pans, then transfer to a plate or an airtight container for storage. At room temperature, the cookies will keep fresh for 3 days; in the freezer, they will keep for 1 month.

LITTLE MOTIVATORS

Makes 12 to 18 cookies

These fudgy, craggy cookies are as much about the nuts and kick of coffee as they are about the insanely deep chocolate cookie dough that barely (in a good way) binds them together. They're chock-full of energy (whether your poison is protein or caffeine) and may make you feel like you're ready to take on the world … or simply motivate you to eat the whole batch before anyone else asks you to share.

→ The nuts in this recipe are unsalted and unroasted. Nuts can go bad quickly, so don't forget to taste yours before using and store them in the fridge or freezer.

→ Nescafé is a great choice for the instant espresso powder.

150g	sugar	¾ cup
84g	unsalted butter, softened	6 T
2	large eggs	
12g	vanilla extract	1 T
395g	chocolate chips	2⅓ cups, divided
70g	flour	½ cup
4g	instant espresso powder	1 T
4g	baking powder	1 tsp
6g	kosher salt	1½ tsp
165g	walnuts, chopped	1½ cups
165g	pecans, chopped	1½ cups

1. Heat the oven to 350°F. Pan-spray or line two half-sheet pans with parchment paper or silicone baking mats.

2. In the bowl of a stand mixer fitted with the paddle attachment, cream together the sugar and butter on medium-high for 2 to 3 minutes until well combined. Scrape down the sides of the bowl, add the eggs and vanilla, and beat until smooth.

3. In a microwave-safe bowl, melt 225g (1⅓ cups) of the chocolate chips in the microwave in 30-second spurts, stirring after each, until smooth. With the mixer on low, add the melted chocolate to the mixture until combined.

4. With the mixer still on low, add the flour, espresso powder, baking powder, and salt. Mix just until the dough comes together, no longer than 1 minute. Scrape down the sides of the bowl with a spatula.

5. Paddle in the remaining 170g (1 cup) chocolate chips, the walnuts, and the pecans, just until incorporated.

6. Using a 2¾-ounce cookie scoop (or a ⅓-cup measure), scoop the dough onto the prepared pans 2 to 3 inches apart. Flatten the domed tops with your palm (it will be a bit sticky, don't worry).

7. Bake at 350°F for 10 to 12 minutes. You won't be able to see much of a visual change to the dough, so make sure to set a timer.

8. Let the cookies cool briefly on the pans, then transfer to a plate or an airtight container for storage. At room temperature, the cookies will keep fresh for 3 days; in the freezer, they will keep for 1 month.

SUGAR SUGAR COOKIES

Makes 12 to 18 cookies

Typically, our recipe creation process starts with a single point of flavor inspiration. Maybe it's a childhood food memory, a classic flavor combination, or a curiosity about how two ingredients would work together. But every so often, the starting point has little to do with flavor at all, as is the case with these Sugar Sugar Cookies, whose inspo is all about texture. A plain Jane sugar cookie is fine—what's not to love about a classic?—but the magic that comes when you add a bit of coarse sugar to the equation is hard to beat. The gritty crunch brings the experience up, up, and away. Round that out with the creaminess of white chocolate chips, and these babes are unstoppable.

250g	sugar	1¼ cups
226g	unsalted butter, softened	2 sticks (16 T)
55g	light brown sugar	¼ cup (packed)
1	large egg	
2g	vanilla extract	½ tsp
290g	flour	2 cups
6g	kosher salt	1½ tsp
2g	baking powder	½ tsp
1.5g	baking soda	¼ tsp
340g	white chocolate chips	2 cups (12 oz bag)
50g	colored sugar	5 T

1. Heat the oven to 350°F. Pan-spray or line two half-sheet pans with parchment paper or silicone baking mats.

2. In the bowl of a stand mixer fitted with the paddle attachment, cream together the sugar, butter, and brown sugar, on medium-high for 4 minutes until well combined. Scrape down the sides of the bowl, add the egg and vanilla, and mix for 4 more minutes.

3. Add the flour, salt, baking powder, and baking soda and paddle on low speed until just combined, about 20 seconds.

4. Paddle in the white chocolate chips and 30g (3 tablespoons) of the colored sugar until just incorporated.

5. Using a 2¾-ounce cookie scoop (or a ⅓-cup measure), scoop the dough onto the prepared pans 2 to 3 inches apart. Sprinkle with the remaining colored sugar.

6. Bake at 350°F until lightly golden around the edges, 8 to 10 minutes.

7. Let the cookies cool briefly on the pans, then transfer to a plate or an airtight container for storage. At room temperature, the cookies will keep fresh for 3 days; in the freezer, they will keep for 1 month.

CHEESECAKE COOKIES

Makes 12 cookies

I fell in love with baking far before it occurred to me that I could make it a profession. My earliest baking memories were standing side by side with my grandmother, great-aunt, and mother in the kitchen, wide-eyed, sneaking a bite of dough every chance I got. From there I moved on to a more…independent study, centered heavily around Jell-O No Bake Cheesecake kits. I would toss the poor excuse for a graham cracker crust aside and devote all my attention to the otherworldly creation that manifested when I spooned together the powdered cheesecake mixture and milk. Wonderfully gooey, this not-at-all-actual cheesecake filling was somehow "baked" enough to safely eat by the spoonful, which I did happily. A lifetime obsession with questionably underbaked cream cheese desserts was born.

→ The citric acid in this recipe rounds out the flavor of the cheesecake. Most of our favorite desserts include secret weapon ingredients we don't even know exist, like this one. Remember, a little goes a long way. Read more on the marvelous powers of citric acid on page 14.

→ This recipe asks you to bake your cookies on parchment paper or a silicone baking mat so the tasty little graham crumbs hugged around your cookie have a place to latch on during baking. It also makes releasing the cookies after baking and cooling a cinch.

→ For the jam swirl, I recommend raspberry or cherry.

270g	sugar	1⅓ cups
113g	unsalted butter, softened	1 stick (8 T)
113g	cream cheese, softened	4 oz
1	large egg yolk	
6g	vanilla extract	1½ tsp
155g	flour	1 cup + 2 T
20g	cornstarch	2 T
6g	milk powder	1 T
4g	kosher salt	1 tsp
1g	baking powder	¼ tsp
0.5g	baking soda	⅛ tsp
0.5g	citric acid	⅛ tsp
1 recipe	Graham Crumbs (recipe follows)	
240g	jam	¾ cup

1. Heat the oven to 350°F. Line two half-sheet pans with parchment paper or silicone baking mats.

2. In the bowl of a stand mixer fitted with the paddle attachment, cream together the sugar and butter on medium-high for 2 to 3 minutes until well combined. Scrape down the sides of the bowl, add the cream cheese, and mix to combine. Scrape the bowl, add the egg yolk and vanilla, and mix for 2 more minutes.

3. Add the flour, cornstarch, milk powder, salt, baking powder, baking soda, and citric acid and paddle on low speed until just combined, about 20 seconds. Put the bowl of dough in the fridge to chill for 10 minutes.

4. Scoop 1 tablespoon of the graham crumbs onto a parchment-lined sheet pan, then scoop a little less than ¼ cup of cheesecake cookie dough on top. Repeat with the remaining crumbs and cookie dough. Scoop 1 tablespoon jam atop each and swirl the dough and jam together with a fork.

5. Bake at 350°F until lightly golden, 10 to 12 minutes.

6. Cool completely on the pans before serving. Transfer the cookies to a plate or an airtight container for storage. At room temperature, the cookies will keep fresh for 3 days; in the freezer, they will keep for 1 month.

GRAHAM CRUMBS
Makes about ½ cup

100g	graham crackers	4 full crackers
25g	sugar	2 T
3g	milk powder	2 tsp
28g	unsalted butter, melted	2 T

1. In a blender or food processor (or in a plastic bag with a rolling pin), pulverize the graham crackers. Measure out ½ cup of crumbs and transfer to a small bowl.

2. Mix the graham cracker crumbs with the sugar and milk powder to combine. Stir in the melted butter until small clusters form evenly across the mixture. Use immediately or store in an airtight container for up to 1 month.

BUTTERSCOTCH PECAN PUDDING COOKIES

Makes 12 cookies

Warm, deep, and packed with memories of Grandma's house, butterscotch brings infinite calm, cozy vibes. These attributes make butterscotch a legend in flavor story potential, but typically you have to use butterscotch chips to do all the heavy lifting. Nothing against a chip-laden cookie, but they can fall short in the luscious, buttery, and rich departments, when you want the cookie itself to shine. To make these cookies really sing, we use a box of butterscotch pudding mix as the secret weapon. It carries incredible flavor through but also adds a soft, almost underbaked layer to the center of every cookie. They're a total knockout.

150g	pecans, roughly chopped	1 cup
140g	unsalted butter, melted	10 T
100g	sugar	½ cup
96g	instant butterscotch pudding mix	1 box (½ cup)
70g	light brown sugar	⅓ cup
1	large egg	
1	egg yolk	
6g	vanilla extract	1½ tsp
215g	flour	1½ cups
6g	kosher salt	1½ tsp
3g	baking soda	½ tsp
170g	butterscotch chips	1 cup

1. Heat the oven to 400°F. Pan-spray or line two half-sheet pans with parchment paper or silicone baking mats.

2. As the oven heats up, spread the pecans on one of the baking sheets and toast 10 to 15 minutes, until nutty and a deep golden brown under the skin. Remove the nuts to a bowl and set the pan aside to be reused.

3. In the bowl of a stand mixer fitted with the paddle attachment, combine the melted butter, sugar, instant pudding mix, and brown sugar and paddle together on medium-high for 2 to 3 minutes until well combined. Scrape down the sides of the bowl, add the whole egg, egg yolk, and vanilla, and beat again until smooth.

4. Add the flour, salt, and baking soda and paddle on low speed just until the dough comes together, no longer than 1 minute. Scrape down the sides of the bowl with a spatula.

5. Paddle in the butterscotch chips and toasted pecans, just until incorporated.

6. Using a 2¾-ounce cookie scoop (or a ⅓-cup measure), scoop the dough onto the prepared pans, 6 scoops per pan, 4 inches apart.

7. Bake at 400°F until still mounded, dry on the edges, and shiny on top, 6 to 8 minutes.

8. Let the cookies cool on the pans for just 5 minutes, then transfer to a plate so they stop cooking from the baking sheet's residual heat while they cool. Once cooled completely, use an airtight container for storage. At room temperature, the cookies will keep fresh for 3 days; in the freezer, they will keep for 1 month.

MARBLED CHOCOLATE S'MORE COOKIES

Makes 12 to 18 cookies

Marshmallow Fluff is one of those hilarious secret pantry items that can make any recipe feel elevated and playful at the same time. Yes, marshmallows studded into a chocolate cookie are pretty awesome, but ribbons of white cloudlike sweetness swirled together with a rich chocolate dough turn your cookie into a work of art. A pop of graham cracker connects the cookie to the sticky moments of your childhood in a way that reminds you that "kid" is just a state of mind.

226g	unsalted butter, softened	2 sticks (16 T)
300g	sugar	1½ cups
1	large egg	
4g	vanilla extract	1 tsp
210g	chocolate chips	1¼ cups, divided
100g	flour	¾ cup
65g	cocoa powder	¾ cup
6g	kosher salt	1½ tsp
4g	baking powder	1 tsp
2g	baking soda	½ tsp
45g	graham crackers, broken in quarter-size chunks	¾ cup
80g	Marshmallow Fluff	⅔ cup

1. Heat the oven to 350°F. Pan-spray or line two half-sheet pans with parchment paper or silicone baking mats.

2. In the bowl of a stand mixer fitted with the paddle attachment, cream together the butter and sugar on medium-high for 2 to 3 minutes until well combined. Scrape down the sides of the bowl, add the egg and vanilla, and mix for 2 more minutes.

3. In a microwave-safe bowl, melt 40g (¼ cup) of the chocolate chips in the microwave in 30-second spurts, stirring after each, until smooth. With the mixer on low, add the melted chocolate and paddle until combined, about 30 seconds.

4. Add the flour, cocoa powder, salt, baking powder, and baking soda and paddle on low speed until just combined, about 1 minute.

5. Paddle in the remaining 170g (1 cup) chocolate chips and broken-up graham crackers until just combined.

6. Scoop in the Marshmallow Fluff and mix on medium speed for 10 seconds.

7. Using a 2¾-ounce cookie scoop (or a ⅓-cup measure), scoop the dough onto the prepared pans 2 to 3 inches apart. Use the palm of your hand to flatten the domes.

8. Bake at 350°F for 8 to 10 minutes.

9. Let the cookies cool briefly on the pans, then transfer to a plate or an airtight container for storage. At room temperature, the cookies will keep fresh for 3 days; in the freezer, they will keep for 1 month.

PEACHY SHORTCAKE COOKIES

Makes 12 to 18 cookies

In the Dessert Hall of Fame (caps because this is obviously a real place), shortcake reigns supreme. Buttery, sweet, fluffy, and flaky at the same time, with some fruit (yes, strawberries, but by no means does it stop there), this dessert cannot be topped. I'm always in pursuit of getting more shortcake into my life (which is why I created a strawberry shortcake soft serve at Milk Bar), but these buttery, fruit-studded peach shortcake cookies are for when I'm off the clock.

→ Clear vanilla extract is key to the whipped creamy note of the epic dessert that inspired this cookie. Read more on page 15.

→ This recipe calls for dried peaches, but dried strawberries, mangoes, heck, even pineapple would be killer.

226g	unsalted butter, softened	2 sticks (16 T)
200g	sugar	1 cup
110g	light brown sugar	½ cup (packed)
1	large egg	
4g	clear vanilla extract	1 tsp
290g	flour	2 cups
6g	kosher salt	1½ tsp
2g	baking powder	½ tsp
1.5g	baking soda	¼ tsp
80g	dried peaches, cut into ¼-inch pieces	1 cup
1 recipe	Shortcake Crumbs (recipe follows)	
200g	turbinado sugar	1 cup

1. Heat the oven to 350°F. Pan-spray or line two half-sheet pans with parchment paper or silicone baking mats.

2. In the bowl of a stand mixer fitted with the paddle attachment, cream together the butter, sugar, and brown sugar on medium-high for 2 to 3 minutes until well combined. Scrape down the sides of the bowl, add the egg and vanilla, and beat until smooth.

3. Add the flour, salt, baking powder, and baking soda and paddle on low speed until just combined, about 20 seconds.

4. Paddle in the dried peaches and shortcake crumbs until just incorporated.

5. Using a 2¾-ounce cookie scoop (or a ⅓-cup measure), scoop the dough onto the prepared pans 2 to 3 inches apart. Use the palm of your hand to flatten the domes. Top each cookie with 1 tablespoon of turbinado sugar.

6. Bake at 350°F until golden around the edges, 10 to 12 minutes.

7. Let the cookies cool briefly on the pans, then transfer to a plate or an airtight container for storage. At room temperature, the cookies will keep fresh for 3 days; in the freezer, they will keep for 1 month.

(recipe continues)

SHORTCAKE CRUMBS

Makes 2 cups

145g	flour	1 cup
50g	sugar	¼ cup
4g	kosher salt	1 tsp
1g	baking powder	¼ tsp
42g	unsalted butter, melted	3 T
24g	vegetable oil	2 T
4g	vanilla extract	1 tsp

1. Heat the oven to 300°F. Pan-spray or line a half-sheet pan with parchment paper or a silicone baking mat.

2. In a medium bowl or stand mixer, mix together the flour, sugar, salt, and baking powder.

3. Add the melted butter, oil, and vanilla to the dry ingredients and toss until small clusters form. Spread the mixture out in one layer on the sheet pan.

4. Bake at 300°F until medium golden brown, about 20 minutes.

5. Cool completely before using. Stored in an airtight container, the crumbs will keep fresh for 1 week at room temperature or 1 month in the fridge or freezer.

CTC MARSH COOKIES

Makes 12 to 18 cookies

We love Cinnamon Toast Crunch so much that we lovingly call it CTC and happily fold it into as many creations as possible—I'm talking pie, frosting, cereal milk, really, we've done it all—when we aren't unabashedly eating it by the handful. Toasting the cereal before adding it to the dough adds depth to the already dreamy flavor. Combine that with the bounce of marshmallows and the creaminess of white chocolate coated in cinnamon, and these cookies take that CTC glory into the stratosphere.

→ If you're not a CTC fan, feel free to sub in your favorite cereal or any combo of cereals you have in the pantry. This cookie recipe is epic with them all. Use your intuition to determine whether toasting the cereal of your choice will deepen the flavor (no to fruity flavors, yes to Frosted Flakes, etc.). I also recommend adjusting sugar varieties (e.g., all granulated sugar for Cap'n Crunch) and chocolate chip flavors (milk chocolate chips for Cookie Crisp) based on the cereal you swap with.

90g	Cinnamon Toast Crunch cereal	2 cups + more for topping
226g	unsalted butter, softened	2 sticks (16 T)
150g	light brown sugar	⅔ cup (packed)
140g	sugar	⅔ cup
1	large egg	
310g	flour	2 cups + 2 T
20g	milk powder	¼ cup
6g	kosher salt	1½ tsp
1.5g	baking soda	¼ tsp
1g	baking powder	¼ tsp
80g	mini marshmallows	1½ cups
1 recipe	Cinnamon Chips (recipe follows)	

1. Heat the oven to 300°F.

2. Spread 90g (2 cups) of the Cinnamon Toast Crunch on a baking sheet and toast in the oven until fragrant, about 10 minutes. Cool completely.

3. Increase the oven temperature to 350°F. Pan-spray or line two half-sheet pans with parchment paper or silicone baking mats.

4. In the bowl of a stand mixer fitted with the paddle attachment, cream together the butter, brown sugar, and sugar on medium-high for 2 to 3 minutes until well combined. Scrape down the sides of the bowl, add the egg, and beat until smooth.

5. Add the flour, milk powder, salt, baking soda, and baking powder and paddle on low speed until just combined, about 20 seconds.

6. Paddle in the toasted cereal and mini marshmallows until just incorporated.

7. Add the cinnamon chips to the dough mixture and mix until homogeneous.

8. Using a 2¾-ounce cookie scoop (or a ⅓-cup measure), scoop the dough onto the prepared pans 2 to 3 inches apart. Use the palm of your hand to flatten the domes. Add 2 to 3 pieces of untoasted cereal to the top of each cookie round.

9. Bake at 350°F until golden brown, 10 to 12 minutes.

10. Let the cookies cool briefly on the pans, then transfer to a plate or an airtight container for storage. At room temperature, the cookies will keep fresh for 3 days; in the freezer, they will keep for 1 month.

(recipe continues)

CINNAMON CHIPS
Makes ½ cup

85g	white chocolate chips	½ cup
2g	vegetable oil	½ tsp
4g	ground cinnamon	2 tsp

In a small bowl, toss the white chocolate chips with the oil, then sprinkle in the cinnamon and toss to coat the chips evenly.

CHERRY PIE COOKIES

Makes 18 cookies

Listen, no shade intended, but nine out of ten days I don't have the time to fuss with pie. Even for a notorious corner-cutter like me, the simplest pie crust can require more attention than I am willing to spend on a sunny summer day. Enter the pie crumb: basically just all the ingredients for pie dough baked into a crumble you don't have to form. It's the most flavorful way to get pie vibes in your life without racking up any time pulsing, chilling, rolling, and pinching in the kitchen—add a few cups of your fave dried fruit, bake it into some cookie dough, and you're a shoo-in for the blue ribbon at the county fair.

→ Sub in other dried fruits if you're more of an apple or blueberry or coconut cream pie kinda person.

→ Add ½ teaspoon of your favorite ground spices for extra edge. (It's not my pref, but it might be yours!)

113g	unsalted butter, softened	1 stick (8 T)
80g	sugar	⅓ cup + 2 tsp
70g	light brown sugar	⅓ cup (packed)
1	large egg	
145g	flour	1 cup
3g	kosher salt	¾ tsp
1g	baking powder	¼ tsp
1g	baking soda	⅛ tsp
1 recipe	Pie Crumbs (recipe follows)	
130g	dried cherries	¾ cup
1	large egg white	
45g	turbinado sugar, for topping	¼ cup

1. In the bowl of a stand mixer fitted with the paddle attachment, cream together the butter, sugar, and brown sugar on medium-high for 2 to 3 minutes until well combined. Scrape down the sides of the bowl, add the egg, and beat for 7 to 8 minutes until well combined.

2. Add the flour, salt, baking powder, and baking soda and paddle on low speed until the dough comes together, no longer than 1 minute. (Do not walk away from the machine during this step, or you will risk overmixing the dough.) Scrape down the sides of the bowl with a spatula.

3. Still on low speed, add the pie crumbs and mix until they're incorporated, no more than 30 seconds. Chase the pie crumbs with the dried cherries, mixing them in for 30 seconds.

4. Using a 2¾-ounce cookie scoop (or a ⅓-cup measure), scoop the dough onto a parchment-lined sheet pan. Use the palm of your hand to flatten the domes. Brush the surface of each flattened round with egg white and sprinkle the turbinado sugar on top. Wrap the sheet pan tightly in plastic wrap and refrigerate for at least 1 hour (or up to 1 week). Do not bake your cookies from room temperature—they will not bake properly.

5. Heat the oven to 350°F. Pan-spray or line two half-sheet pans with parchment paper or silicone baking mats.

6. Arrange the chilled dough rounds a minimum of 4 inches apart on the pans.

7. Bake at 350°F until the cookies puff, crackle, and spread, 8 to 10 minutes. They should be very faintly browned on the edges yet still bright yellow in the center; give them an extra minute or so if that's not the case.

8. Let the cookies cool completely on the pans, then transfer to a plate or an airtight container for storage. At room temperature, the cookies will keep fresh for 5 days; in the freezer, they will keep for 1 month.

PIE CRUMBS
Makes 1⅓ cups

110g	flour	¾ cup
13g	sugar	1 T
2g	kosher salt	½ tsp
56g	unsalted butter, melted and cooled	4 T
12g	vegetable oil	1 T

1. Heat the oven to 350°F. Pan-spray or line a half-sheet pan with parchment paper or a silicone baking mat.

2. In the bowl of a stand mixer fitted with the paddle attachment, combine the flour, sugar, and salt and paddle on low speed until well mixed, 15 to 30 seconds.

3. Add the melted butter and oil and paddle on low speed until the mixture starts to come together in small clusters, 15 to 30 seconds. Spread the clusters on the prepared sheet pan.

4. Bake at 350°F for 25 minutes, breaking them up occasionally. The crumbs should be deeper than golden brown and still slightly moist to the touch at that point; they will dry and harden as they cool.

5. Let the crumbs cool completely before using in a recipe or eating. Stored in an airtight container, the crumbs will keep fresh for 1 week at room temperature or 1 month in the fridge or freezer.

STRAWBERRY SHORTCAKE COOKIES

Makes 16 cookies

Chocolate, vanilla, marbled, yellow—cookies come in a rainbow. I mean, what's the point of life if it's not in Technicolor?! These pink ladies get their hue and flavor from the freeze-dried strawberry powder, which makes them tangy, bright, and easy on the eyes. White chocolate chips and shortcake crumbs give the cookie creaminess and different textures, proving that sometimes it is what's inside *and* outside that counts.

→ You can get freeze-dried strawberry powder online, or you can buy freeze-dried strawberries and grind them down in a blender.

→ Citric acid helps make these pink babes have that fresh fruit taste. Read up on it on page 14.

266g	unsalted butter, softened	2 sticks (16 T)
400g	sugar	2 cups
1	large egg	
0.75 g	red food coloring	¼ tsp
255g	flour	1¾ cups
18g	freeze-dried strawberry powder	¼ cup + 2 T
6g	baking soda	1½ tsp
4g	baking powder	1 tsp
4g	kosher salt	1 tsp
0.5g	citric acid	⅛ tsp
170g	white chocolate chips	1 cup
120g	Shortcake Crumbs (page 114)	1 cup

1. Heat the oven to 350°F. Pan-spray or line two half-sheet pans with parchment paper or silicone baking mats.

2. In the bowl of a stand mixer fitted with the paddle attachment, cream together the butter and sugar on medium-high for 2 to 3 minutes, until well combined. Scrape down the sides of the bowl, add the egg and food coloring, and beat until smooth.

3. Add the flour, dried strawberry powder, baking soda, baking powder, salt, and citric acid. Paddle on low speed until just combined, about 20 seconds. (This dough can be crumbly, so be sure to mix until it comes together.)

4. Paddle in the white chocolate chips and shortcake crumbs until just incorporated.

5. Using a 2¾-ounce cookie scoop (or a ⅓-cup measure), scoop the dough onto the prepared pans 2 to 3 inches apart. Use the palm of your hand to slightly flatten the domes.

6. Bake at 350°F until golden around the edges, 8 to 10 minutes.

7. Let the cookies cool briefly on the pans, then transfer to a plate or an airtight container for storage. At room temperature, the cookies will keep fresh for 3 days; in the freezer, they will keep for 1 month.

PRETZEL CHOCOLATE CHUNK COOKIES

Makes 12 to 18 cookies

At Milk Bar, we have a saying inspired by our iconically larger-than-life dresser/CMO, Sarah Tabb: More is more. We don't do it every day. We're not the rainbow-frosted, sprinkle-filled, doodad-covered everything bakery. But every so often we get a voice in our heads that says: MORE. These cookies are living the loud and proud lifestyle. At their base they are a responsible, well-balanced, deep, and soulful cookie, but we plussed them up with salty pretzels and luxurious chocolate, and topped the whole thing with flaky sea salt—and we're not even sorry.

→ 55% (aka milk) chocolate really makes these dreamy, but if you KNOW you're a dark chocolate–covered pretzel person, feel free to substitute.

100g	mini pretzels	2 cups, divided
115g	55% chocolate	4 oz
226g	unsalted butter, softened	2 sticks (16 T)
280g	dark brown sugar	1¼ cups (packed)
170g	light brown sugar	¾ cup (packed)
1	large egg	
7g	molasses	1 tsp
2g	vanilla extract	½ tsp
256g	flour	1¾ cups
8g	kosher salt	2 tsp
4g	baking powder	1 tsp
2g	baking soda	½ tsp
2g	flaky salt, for topping	1 tsp

1. Heat the oven to 350°F. Pan-spray or line two half-sheet pans with parchment paper or silicone baking mats.

2. In a food processor or blender, grind 50g (1 heaping cup) of the pretzels to a powder and set aside. Roughly chop the chocolate with a knife to the size of a dime and smaller (variety is great here) and set aside.

3. In the bowl of a stand mixer fitted with the paddle attachment, cream together the butter, dark brown sugar, and light brown sugar on medium-high for 4 minutes until well combined. Scrape down the sides of the bowl, add the egg, molasses, and vanilla and mix for 4 more minutes.

4. Add the flour, ground pretzels, salt, baking powder, and baking soda and paddle on low speed until just combined, about 20 seconds.

5. Paddle in the remaining 50g (1 cup) of whole pretzels and reserved chopped chocolate until just incorporated.

6. Using a 2¾-ounce cookie scoop (or a ⅓-cup measure), scoop the dough onto the prepared pans 2 to 3 inches apart. Flatten the domed tops with your palm. Sprinkle flaky salt on top.

7. Bake at 350°F until brown, 8 to 10 minutes.

8. Let the cookies cool on the sheet pans. Store in an airtight container with a slice of bread for maximum fudginess for up to 3 days.

CINNAMON BUN COOKIES

Makes 18 cookies

I believe firmly in the power of making new traditions and that something-to-look-forward-to feeling that can come from even an everyday task when it's performed with intention and warmth. Cinnamon rolls are a Christmas Day tradition for me—no matter where the holidays take me, I bake 'em by the trayful for friends and fam to crush in the fury of opening presents and the lazy morning that usually follows. The smells of cinnamon and sugar and cream cheese frosting transport me to those happy mornings, and these cookies are my way of bringing that joy into the other 364 days of the year—opening presents optional.

226g	unsalted butter, softened	2 sticks (16 T)
140g	sugar	⅔ cup
115g	light brown sugar	½ cup (packed)
1	large egg	
8g	vanilla extract	2 tsp
310g	flour	2 cups + 2 T
20g	milk powder	¼ cup
6g	kosher salt	1½ tsp
2g	baking powder	½ tsp
1g	baking soda	⅛ tsp
6g	ground cinnamon	1 T
168g	cream cheese	6 oz

1. Heat the oven to 350°F. Pan-spray or line two half-sheet pans with parchment paper or silicone baking mats.

2. In the bowl of a stand mixer fitted with the paddle attachment, cream together the butter, sugar, and brown sugar on medium-high for 2 to 3 minutes until well combined. Scrape down the sides of the bowl, add the egg and vanilla, and mix for 2 more minutes.

3. Add the flour, milk powder, salt, baking powder, and baking soda and paddle on low speed until combined, about 1 minute.

4. Divide the dough in half. Knead the cinnamon into one half of the dough.

5. Fill a 2-ounce cookie scoop (or ¼-cup measure) half full with cinnamon dough and the remaining half with plain dough. Pinch and twist the doughs together with your fingers to form a swirl. Flip the cookie dough ball upside down. Using your thumbs, create a well big enough to hide 1 tablespoon of cream cheese inside, then wrap the cookie dough edges around to seal entirely.

6. Place the dough rounds seam-side down on the prepared pans 2 to 3 inches apart. Use the palm of your hand to flatten the dough.

7. Bake at 350°F until golden brown around the edges, 8 to 10 minutes.

8. Let cool on the pan (they're AWESOME warm) or store in an airtight container in the fridge for up to 1 week.

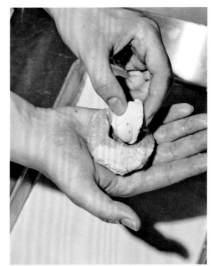
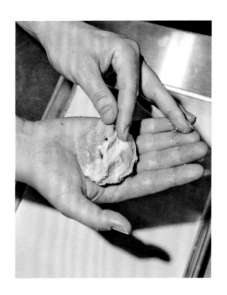

RITZ CRACKER COOKIES

Makes 12 cookies

A version of this cookie—with the crackers folded directly into the cookie dough—has been in my life for a few decades now, and yet every time a batch comes out of the oven I fall in love all over again. The butter-on-butter action of the sugar cookie base on the Ritz crackers is the exact right amount of over the top—with some milk powder to round out the edges. These cookies are downright great on their own, but I wouldn't be mad if you smeared on a jam or subbed them into your cheese plate.

→ This recipe will translate with other crackers. But let's get serious, is there really a BETTER cracker than the Ritz? I'd be super impressed if you subbed in some Ritz PB sandwich crackers, though.

226g	unsalted butter, softened	2 sticks (16 T)
350g	sugar	1¾ cups
1	large egg	
215g	flour	1½ cups
20g	milk powder	¼ cup
6g	kosher salt	1½ tsp
3g	baking powder	¾ tsp
1.5g	baking soda	¼ tsp
116g	Ritz crackers, crushed slightly	1 sleeve + 5 more (2 cups, crushed)

1. Heat the oven to 350°F. Pan-spray or line two half-sheet pans with parchment paper or silicone baking mats.

2. In the bowl of a stand mixer fitted with the paddle attachment, cream together the butter and sugar on medium-high for 2 to 3 minutes until well combined. Scrape down the sides of the bowl, add the egg, and mix for 2 more minutes.

3. Add the flour, milk powder, salt, baking powder, and baking soda and paddle on low speed until just combined, about 20 seconds.

4. Add the crackers and mix until well incorporated. You want your crackers to break down into smaller pieces as you mix, but you don't want cracker dust.

5. Using a 2¾-ounce cookie scoop (or a ⅓-cup measure), scoop the dough onto the prepared pans 2 to 3 inches apart.

6. Bake at 350°F until golden around the edges, 8 to 10 minutes.

7. Let the cookies cool briefly on the pans. Share immediately unless you have enviable self-control. If you do have cookies left over, store them in an airtight container with a slice of bread for up to 5 days for maximum fudginess.

CHIPLESS WONDERS

Makes 12 to 18 cookies

I was introduced to this cookie as a kid, spending summers on my grandma's farm. My aunt Sylv picked us up and had two Cool Whip containers in the center seat, both filled with cookies. "Here," she said. "Don't know if you're a Chipless Wonder like Steve, or a Chipfull gal like Rachie." This wonder woman had a house divided: Half her family demanded cookies with chocolate chips, the others, without. Every time she made cookies, she had to make two batches! I had never even conceived of a chocolate chip cookie without the creamy dotted bites of chocolate, but one warm vanilla-y Chipless Wonder turned into two. And as they say, the rest is history.

Also, it felt impossible to write a cookie book without a chocolate chip cookie recipe, so add as many or as few chocolate chips as you'd like if you're a Chipfull kind of cookie spirit….

226g	unsalted butter, softened	2 sticks (16 T)
170g	light brown sugar	¾ cup (packed)
100g	sugar	½ cup
1	large egg	
8g	vanilla extract	2 tsp
290g	flour	2 cups
12g	milk powder	2 T
5g	kosher salt	1¼ tsp
2g	baking powder	½ tsp
1g	baking soda	¼ tsp

1. In the bowl of a stand mixer fitted with the paddle attachment, cream together the butter, brown sugar, and sugar on medium-high for 2 to 3 minutes until well combined. Scrape down the sides of the bowl, add the egg and vanilla, and beat for 7 to 8 minutes until combined.

2. Add the flour, milk powder, salt, baking powder and baking soda and paddle on low speed until just combined, no longer than 1 minute. (Do not walk away from the machine during this step or you will risk overmixing the dough.) Scrape down the sides of the bowl with a spatula.

3. Using a 2¾-ounce cookie scoop (or a ⅓-cup measure), scoop the dough onto a parchment-lined sheet pan. Use the palm of your hand to flatten the domes. Wrap the sheet pan tightly in plastic wrap and refrigerate for at least 1 hour. Do not bake your cookies from room temperature—they will not bake properly.

4. Heat the oven to 350°F. Pan-spray or line two half-sheet pans with parchment paper or silicone baking mats.

5. Arrange the chilled dough on the prepared sheet pans a minimum of 4 inches apart.

6. Bake at 350°F until the cookies puff, crackle, and spread, about 10 minutes. They should be golden brown on the edges with a slightly underbaked bull's-eye center; give them an extra minute or so if that's not the case.

7. Let the cookies cool completely on the sheet pans, then transfer to a plate or an airtight container for storage. At room temperature, the cookies will keep fresh for 5 days; in the freezer, they will keep for 1 month.

In the world of cookie science, creaming is VIP—see my real talk on creaming on page 20.

A cookie can go from dense and fudgy perfection to overbaked blah in minutes flat. As you get comfortable baking, you will learn to train your eyes to spot success. IMHO, cookie #3 will make you proud every time.

CHOCOLATE MALTED BROWNIE COOKIES

Makes 24 cookies

Malt flavor is hard to describe. It's that deeply flavorful, sweet, tickle-of-the-tongue moment that transports you back to slurping that as-big-as-your-head chocolate malt at the ice cream shop as a kid. Or the outer-space texture of those crunchy little balls coated in chocolate—a flavor you know with your eyes closed but can't quite put your finger on. A chocolate cookie on its own can come across as rather one-dimensional, but a dense and fudgy brownie cookie with a dash of malted milk powder (okay, so it's technically a flavor combo of barley, wheat, and condensed milk) and you're tasting double—old nostalgic throwbacks and brand-new flavor combos, magical and still seemingly impossible to put into words.

→ If you don't have bittersweet chocolate, sub in semisweet chocolate chips and remove 2 tablespoons of sugar from the mix.

→ Malted milk powder—not to be confused with nonfat milk powder (page 17)—is the secret milky, barley-ish, sweet ingredient in these cookies. The star of the soda shop classic malted milkshake and movie theater standby Whopper candy, malted milk powder can be found in most grocery stores in the powdered drink section. Nestlé makes a great version.

200g	bittersweet chocolate, chopped	7 oz
84g	unsalted butter, softened	6 T
125g	sugar	½ cup + 2 T
75g	light brown sugar	⅓ cup (packed)
2	large eggs, at room temperature	
110g	flour	¾ cup
45g	malted milk powder	⅓ cup + 1½ T
20g	cocoa powder	¼ cup
3g	kosher salt	¾ tsp

1. Heat the oven to 350°F. Pan-spray or line two half-sheet pans with parchment paper or silicone baking mats.

2. In a microwave-safe bowl, combine the chocolate and butter and melt in the microwave in 30-second spurts, stirring after each, until smooth. Set aside to cool to room temperature.

3. In the bowl of a stand mixer fitted with the whisk attachment, whip together the sugar, brown sugar, and eggs on medium-high for 2 to 3 minutes until aerated. Scrape down the sides of the bowl.

4. With the mixer on low, add the melted chocolate/butter mixture, mixing until combined.

5. Add the flour, 35g (⅓ cup) of the malted milk powder, the cocoa powder, and salt and mix on low speed just until the dough comes together, no longer than 1 minute. Scrape down the sides of the bowl with a spatula.

6. Using a ¾-ounce cookie scoop (or mounded tablespoon), scoop the dough onto the prepared pans 2 to 3 inches apart. Top each cookie with a generous pinch of malted milk powder.

7. Bake at 350°F until the cookies are puffed with shiny crackled edges, 6 to 7 minutes. Err on the side of underbaking these for maximum gooey middles!

8. Let the cookies cool completely on the pans. Transfer the cookies to a plate or an airtight container for storage. At room temperature, the cookies will keep fresh for 3 days; in the freezer, they will keep for 1 month.

NANA NILLAS

Makes 12 cookies

There is a reason that home cooks and beloved bakeries alike have been whipping up batches of banana pudding studded with vanilla cookies for decades—the simple combination is irresistible. There is no scientific explanation for why these two humdrum items become otherworldly when layered up in a trifle-like creation, but the results are indisputable—so much so that I needed to hack the equation and make a cookie that tastes like banana pudding. Banana extract brings the thunder to these more-than-meets-the-eye cookies that might just give that ol' pudding a run for its money.

226g	unsalted butter, softened	2 sticks (16 T)
200g	sugar	1 cup
115g	light brown sugar	½ cup (packed)
1	large egg	
6g	banana extract	1½ tsp
2g	vanilla extract	½ tsp
0.5g	yellow food coloring	10 drops
250g	flour	1¾ cups
6g	kosher salt	1½ tsp
2g	baking powder	½ tsp
1.5g	baking soda	¼ tsp
150g	Nilla wafers	2 cups

1. Heat the oven to 350°F. Pan-spray or line two half-sheet pans with parchment paper or silicone baking mats.

2. In the bowl of a stand mixer fitted with the paddle attachment, cream together the butter, sugar, and brown sugar on medium-high for 2 to 3 minutes until well combined. Scrape down the sides of the bowl, add the egg, banana extract, vanilla, and food coloring and mix for 2 more minutes.

3. Add the flour, salt, baking powder, and baking soda and paddle on low speed until just combined, about 20 seconds.

4. Place the wafers in a freezer bag and seal. Using the palm of your hand, break the wafers into pieces about one-eighth of the original size. Paddle into the dough just until incorporated.

5. Using a 2¾-ounce cookie scoop (or a ⅓-cup measure), scoop the dough onto the prepared pans 2 to 3 inches apart. Flatten the domed tops with your palm.

6. Bake at 350°F until golden around the edges, 8 to 10 minutes.

7. Let the cookies cool briefly on the pans, then transfer to a plate or an airtight container for storage. At room temperature, the cookies will keep fresh for 3 days; in the freezer, they will keep for 1 month.

FRENCH TOAST COOKIES

Makes 12 to 18 cookies

One of the quickest ways to bring a flavor into your cookie is through mix-ins (or as pros call them, "inclusions"). Check out the pie crumbs in the Cherry Pie Cookies (page 118) or the caramelized cereal in the CTC Marsh Cookies (page 115)—these flavorful bits help tell the flavor story and add texture and complexity. When working through the idea for a French toast cookie—something maple-y, buttery, and yeah, okay, BREAD-y—I knew a maple-infused crumble inclusion was the way to go. This re-creates the breakfast-table excitement of staring down at a plate of drippy, soft-in-the-center French toast slices. Which, yes, also means this cookie is great for breakfast.

Oh, and for the record: These crumbs and crumbles always make the best baking snack.

→ Milk powder helps give this cookie its rounded, milky notes. Read up on it on page 17.

226g	unsalted butter, softened	2 sticks (16 T)
180g	light brown sugar	¾ cup (packed)
140g	sugar	⅔ cup + more for coating
2	large eggs	
4g	vanilla extract	1 tsp
310g	flour	2 cups + 2 T
12g	milk powder	2 T
4g	kosher salt	1 tsp
2g	baking powder	½ tsp
1.5g	baking soda	¼ tsp
1 recipe	French Toast Crumble (recipe follows), cooled	

1. Heat the oven to 350°F. Pan-spray or line two half-sheet pans with parchment paper or silicone baking mats.

2. In the bowl of a stand mixer fitted with the paddle attachment, cream together the butter, brown sugar, and sugar on medium-high for 2 to 3 minutes, until well combined. Scrape down the sides of the bowl, add the eggs and vanilla, and beat until smooth.

3. Add the flour, milk powder, salt, baking powder, and baking soda and paddle on low speed until just combined, about 20 seconds.

4. Paddle in the French toast crumble until just incorporated.

5. Using a 2¾-ounce cookie scoop (or a ⅓-cup measure), scoop the dough onto the prepared pans 2 to 3 inches apart. Use the palm of your hand to slightly flatten the domes.

6. Bake at 350°F until golden around the edges, 10 to 12 minutes.

7. As soon as you pull the cookies out of the oven, flatten their tops once again with a rubber spatula for maximum, memorably fudgy centers. Let the cookies cool briefly on the pans, then transfer to a plate or an airtight container for storage. At room temperature, the cookies will keep fresh for 3 days; in the freezer, they will keep for 1 month.

FRENCH TOAST CRUMBLE

110g	bread of your choice, torn into ½-inch pieces	¼ lb
100g	sugar	½ cup
2g	kosher salt	½ tsp
1g	cinnamon	½ tsp
56g	unsalted butter, melted	4 T
2	large eggs	

1. Heat the oven to 300°F. Pan-spray or line two half-sheet pans with parchment paper or silicone baking mats.

2. In a medium bowl, toss the bread pieces together with the sugar, salt, and cinnamon until evenly coated.

3. In a separate bowl, whisk the butter and eggs together, then toss it into the bread mixture and mix until wet and well coated.

4. Spread the mixture on the prepared baking sheets and bake slow and low at 300°F until golden brown, with a caramelized edge, but leaving some chew in the centers, 45 minutes.

5. Cool completely before using.

CARROT CAKE COOKIES

Makes 12 to 18 cookies

As an adult-ish woman who spends most of her waking time either mixing sugar and butter or thinking about mixing sugar and butter, I like to sneak in a baked good here and there that I can fool myself into thinking is virtuous. Maybe it's my mother's voice perpetually echoing in my head … or the hard-learned lesson that sugar crashes are a very real thing, my friends … but a cookie that adds in veggies—and protein and fruit to boot—is one this undercover grown-up needs in her life. (But don't worry, they are just as irresistible as their less vegetable-y counterparts.)

→ A Microplane is a very, very fine grater. Please don't use the grater you would use to shred carrots for a classic carrot cake, or you will be VERY unhappy with the texture of the cookie.

226g	unsalted butter, softened	2 sticks (16 T)
170g	light brown sugar	¾ cup (packed)
100g	sugar	½ cup
1	large egg	
4g	vanilla extract	1 tsp
65g	carrots, Microplaned (see note above)	⅓ cup
325g	flour	2¼ cups
6g	milk powder	1 T
6g	kosher salt	1½ tsp
2g	ground cinnamon	1 tsp
2g	baking powder	½ tsp
0.5g	baking soda	⅛ tsp
105g	walnuts, toasted and chopped	1 cup
150g	golden raisins	1 cup

1. Heat the oven to 350°F. Pan-spray or line two half-sheet pans with parchment paper or silicone baking mats.

2. In the bowl of a stand mixer fitted with the paddle attachment, cream together the butter, brown sugar, and sugar on medium-high for 2 to 3 minutes until well combined. Scrape down the sides of the bowl, add the egg and vanilla, and mix for 2 more minutes. Add the carrots and mix until well combined.

3. Add the flour, milk powder, salt, cinnamon, baking powder, and baking soda and paddle on low speed until just combined, about 20 seconds.

4. Paddle in the walnuts and raisins just until incorporated.

5. Using a 2¾-ounce cookie scoop (or a ⅓-cup measure), scoop the dough onto the prepared pans 2 to 3 inches apart. Flatten the domed tops with your palm (it will be a bit sticky, don't worry).

6. Bake at 350°F until golden at the edges, 8 to 10 minutes.

7. Let the cookies cool briefly on the pans, then transfer to a plate or an airtight container for storage. At room temperature, the cookies will keep fresh for 3 days; in the freezer, they will keep for 1 month.

LOW BAKES
& NO BAKES

WHEN WE TOOK ON THIS COOKIE BOOK, WE KNEW WE HAD OUR WORK cut out for us. Cookies! It's the biggest subject matter there could be. The pressure was on, and we had to get scholarly. Day one of planning, we asked ourselves a question: What is a cookie? Head scratches and blank stares all around. Every time we narrowed in on some boundaries, we thought of an exception.

"Well, it's some combo of flour, butter, sugar, and eggs made into a dough and baked!"

Was met with:

"…but what about sandies?!"

"…or using oil instead of butter!"

"…not all cookies have eggs. Like shortbread."

It went like this until we got to the point where we couldn't even agree on the fact that a treat needed to be baked to be considered a cookie.

This ambiguity is perhaps why, of all the baked goods under the sun, cookies call to me the most. They break all rules. They live life on their own terms. They dare you to box them in. Cookies are in the eye of the beholder. Let's push the boundaries even further: Set your oven as low as it can go or ditch it completely—we're digging into the world of meringues and beyond. I won't tell if you won't.

MILKFLAKE CRISP

Makes 16 pieces

While I try not to spend too much time mindlessly scrolling through social media—two minutes can quickly lead to two hours when I find good tiny house or DIY accounts—it has become a brilliant source of baking inspiration. Whether I am having my mind blown by Bake Club's most recent recipe takes or virtually eating my way through the whole menu of a burger shack halfway across the country, my creativity cup is constantly refilled by digital strangers. One such sugar-filled rabbit hole led me to this recipe. A favorite of Asian-cuisine-focused content creators, Taiwanese snowflake crisp is like a Rice Krispies Treat's well-traveled cousin, oozing with flair. They're usually made with crushed crackers or cookies, marshmallows, butter, and milk powder, with some dried fruit and nuts. Every time I take a bite of this flaky and chewy nougat-ish creation, I thank the algorithm for bringing us together. This is our version!

→ The possibilities are endless with this highly adaptable treat: Swap in dried fruit, nuts, cookies even!

→ You know I have a thing for adding milk powder (see page 17) to recipes, but this one traditionally calls for it, even further proof we were meant for each other. The milk powder enhances the chew and depth of flavor—don't leave it out!

→ You can also rock this recipe in the microwave as you might a traditional Rice Krispies Treat. Just make sure you work quickly or give the batter a few seconds of heat bursts in between ingredient additions if it cools off.

	milk powder, for dusting the pan	
113g	unsalted butter	1 stick (8 T)
283g	mini marshmallows	10 oz bag
80g	milk powder	¾ cup + 2½ T
10g	black sesame seeds	2 tsp
2g	kosher salt	½ tsp
150g	Ritz crackers	46 crackers (1½ sleeves)
125g	dried cranberries	1 cup

1. Pan-spray an 8 × 8-inch baking pan and line with a rectangle of parchment with a bit of overhang on two sides (this will be helpful when removing the nougat later). Dust lightly with milk powder.

2. In a large nonstick skillet, melt the butter over low heat. Add the mini marshmallows and cook, stirring constantly, until they melt into a batter, about 1 minute.

3. Stir in the milk powder, sesame seeds, and salt and remove from the heat. Continue stirring to dissolve.

4. Fold the whole Ritz crackers and dried cranberries into the marshmallow batter until well coated.

5. Transfer the mixture to the lined pan. Use a greased spatula to gently smooth down and press the nougat into the corners. Leave to cool completely at room temperature or pop in the refrigerator.

6. Use the parchment overhang to transfer the nougat to a cutting board. Slice into 2-inch squares, or whatever size you prefer! Transfer the nougat to a plate or an airtight container for storage. At room temperature, the nougat will keep fresh for 1 week.

CHOCOLATE PEANUT BUTTER DIAMONDS

Makes 24 pieces + snacks and scraps · V · GF

The Milk Bar banana cake has long been a staff favorite: banana cream, hazelnut crunch, chocolate-hazelnut ganache, and hazelnut frosting—it's not for the faint of heart. I love banana, but the real MVP of that recipe is the nutty crunch, a magical mix of hazelnut praline, toasty flakes of feuilletine (a fancy French thing), and salt. These peanut butter bars are an homage to that particularly magical component of that cake, swapping the feuilletine for ground Rice Krispies cereal for more ease and accessibility. Even easier still: These soon-to-be-favorites don't require an oven at all.

→ Choose vegan chocolate chips if your crowd is entirely dairy-free! If not, the classic chocolate chip will work great!

→ Do you have extra toasted Rice Krispies, but you're not in the mood for a bowl of cereal? Save them to add to Milkflake Crisp (page 144) or top your next batch of macaroni and cheese—just trust me.

→ While these like a few minutes out of the freezer to soften before you demolish them, they don't like to wait all day to be consumed, although personal history tells me this will not be an issue.

95g	Rice Krispies cereal	3½ cups
240g	confectioners' sugar	2 cups
4g	kosher salt	1 tsp
110g	coconut oil or vegan butter	½ cup
295g	creamy peanut butter	1 cup + 3 T, divided
180g	semisweet chocolate chips	1 cup + 1 T
	flaky salt, for topping	

1. Line an 8 × 8-inch square pan with 2 perpendicular pieces of plastic wrap with a few inches hanging over the edges.

2. In a large skillet, toast the Rice Krispies over medium heat until darkly golden and fragrant, about 3 minutes. Transfer to a food processor and grind until broken up like fine bread crumbs.

(Alternatively, place them in a 1-gallon plastic bag and use a rolling pin to crush by hand.) Transfer to a large bowl, add the confectioners' sugar and kosher salt, and whisk together, breaking up any large clumps.

3. In a microwave-safe medium bowl, melt the coconut oil in the microwave in 10-second spurts until liquid. Add 250g (1 cup) of the peanut butter to the melted oil and whisk together until shiny and smooth. Pour the peanut butter mixture into the bowl with the sugar and crumbs and use your hands (truly the best tool!) to squeeze and fold together until big crumbs form.

4. Distribute the crumbs around the plastic-lined pan and press down firmly, filling in all gaps to form a solid layer. Use the flat bottom of a glass or measuring cup to finish smoothing and evening out in small circular motions.

5. In a microwave-safe medium bowl, melt the chocolate chips in the microwave in 30-second spurts, stirring after each, until smooth. Add the remaining 45g (3 tablespoons) of peanut butter to the melted chocolate and stir to combine.

6. Pour the chocolate/peanut butter mixture over the flattened Rice Krispies/peanut butter layer and, using a butter knife or small offset spatula, spread it into a smooth layer corner to corner. Top with a generous amount of flaky salt.

7. Transfer to the freezer uncovered for 40 minutes, or until firm to the touch.

8. Use the plastic overhang to lift the bars out of the pan and onto a cutting board. Tug to remove the plastic wrap from beneath and toss. Let sit at room temperature for 10 minutes to soften.

9. Use a long chef's knife to score the top at 1-inch intervals all the way across. Slice into eight 1 × 8-inch strips. Set one strip at a time in front of you lengthwise and slice at a 45-degree angle in 1½-inch lengths to form diamonds. Serve out of the fridge or freezer! The bars can be wrapped and refrigerated for 1 week or frozen for 1 month.

AIR-FRIED CHOCOLATE CHIP COOKIES À LA MARTINE

Makes 30 cookies

I know, I KNOW I told you Milk Bar would never sell a plain chocolate chip cookie, but this is different. (1) This cookie recipe isn't mine. Like all truly great chocolate chip recipes, this one actually belonged to someone very special to me. Whenever I take a bite, I'm filled with warmth and I know that she's near. (2) This recipe requires no oven. Air fryers have brought fried foods into our daily lives (okay, they were already in mine), but did you know they can be used for baking? This tiny tabletop convection oven will have warm cookies in your hands without needing to heat up the oven—perfect for when you just need a quick, warm cookie hug.

→ Though she never owned an air fryer, I know Martine, the creator of this cookie, would give me both a "lawd" and the coolest head-tilt-single-eyebrow "you never know" nod you crave from one of your heroes.

→ No air fryer but dying to get down? Just bake these on two half-sheet pans (pan-sprayed or lined with parchment paper or silicone baking mats) at 375°F for 10 minutes.

375g	light brown sugar	1⅔ cups (packed)
226g	unsalted butter, softened	2 sticks (16 T)
2	large eggs	
2g	vanilla extract	½ tsp
325g	flour	2¼ cups
8g	kosher salt	1 T
5.5g	baking soda	1⅛ tsp
280g	chocolate chips	1½ cups
	flaky salt, for topping	

1. Heat the air fryer to 270°F.

2. In the bowl of a stand mixer fitted with the paddle attachment, cream together the brown sugar and butter on medium-high for 4 minutes until well combined. Scrape down the sides of the bowl, add the eggs and vanilla, and mix for 4 more minutes. Scrape down the sides of the bowl again.

3. Add the flour, kosher salt, and baking soda and paddle on low speed until just combined, about 20 seconds.

4. Paddle in the chocolate chips until just incorporated.

5. Scoop the dough into 2-tablespoon balls. Line the basket of an air fryer with a square of parchment paper or foil, leaving about ½ inch of space around the sides for air circulation.

6. Evenly space 3 cookie dough balls in the basket and use the palm of your hand to flatten slightly. Sprinkle with flaky salt and bake for 9 to 10 minutes, until the cookies have spread and are puffed throughout. Cool for 5 minutes before removing from the basket. Repeat with the remaining dough, 3 cookies per batch.

7. At room temperature, the cookies will keep fresh for 3 days; in the freezer, they will keep for 1 month.

MERINGUE-A-TANGS

Makes 16 cookies · GF

If you're a veteran of the Milk Bar universe, you know we love a drink powder. Tang in blondies! Lipton tea in an Arnold Palmer Cake! Milk powder in just about anything! Drink powders are a great way to pack in a ton of flavor without adding unwanted liquid, which would affect texture and spread. These meringues may appear dainty and demure, but they pack a wallop of flavor and have proven to be majorly irresistible—plus the low bake temperature makes them great for a summer treat when turning on the oven seems impossible—conveniently, during the ultimate Kool-Aid time of year.

→ Other flavor options to replace the Kool-Aid:

- 30g (2 T) Lipton Iced Tea with Lemon mix
- 18g (1 T) Tang mix + 3 drops orange food coloring
- 6g (1 tsp) lemonade mix + 6 drops yellow food coloring
- 35g (⅓ cup) Strawberry Nesquik powder + 2 drops red food coloring

2	egg whites, at room temperature	
120g	confectioners' sugar	1 cup
1g	kosher salt	¼ tsp
12g	Blue Raspberry Lemonade Kool-Aid mix	1 T
	blue food coloring	3 drops
6g	sprinkles for decorating (optional)	2 tsp

1. Heat the oven to 250°F. Pan-spray or line two half-sheet pans with parchment paper or silicone baking mats.

2. Fill a saucepan with 2 inches of water and bring to a simmer. Choose a metal bowl that fits securely on the saucepan but above the water level, but don't put it in the pan yet. In it, whisk together the egg whites, confectioners' sugar, and salt until smooth.

3. Place the bowl over the saucepan and whisk constantly until the egg white mixture is hot to the touch, about 2 minutes. Whisk in the powdered drink mix and food coloring until dissolved.

4. Transfer the meringue mixture to the bowl of a stand mixer fitted with the whisk attachment. Whip the meringue on high until the mixture becomes glossy, thickens, and forms stiff peaks, about 5 minutes.

5. Quickly transfer the meringue to a zip-seal or piping bag and pipe into kisses about 2 inches wide and 1½ inches tall onto the prepared pans. (Alternatively, use 2 spoons to scoop and scrape drops of the meringue onto the prepared pans.) Top with sprinkles if using.

6. Place the pan in the heated oven and crack the door open with a wooden spoon. Bake at 250°F until the meringues are slightly puffed but haven't taken on any color, about 30 minutes. They should feel dry to the touch and will continue to dry while cooling.

7. Let the cookies cool completely on the pans, then transfer to a plate or an airtight container for storage. At room temperature, the cookies will keep fresh for 1 week.

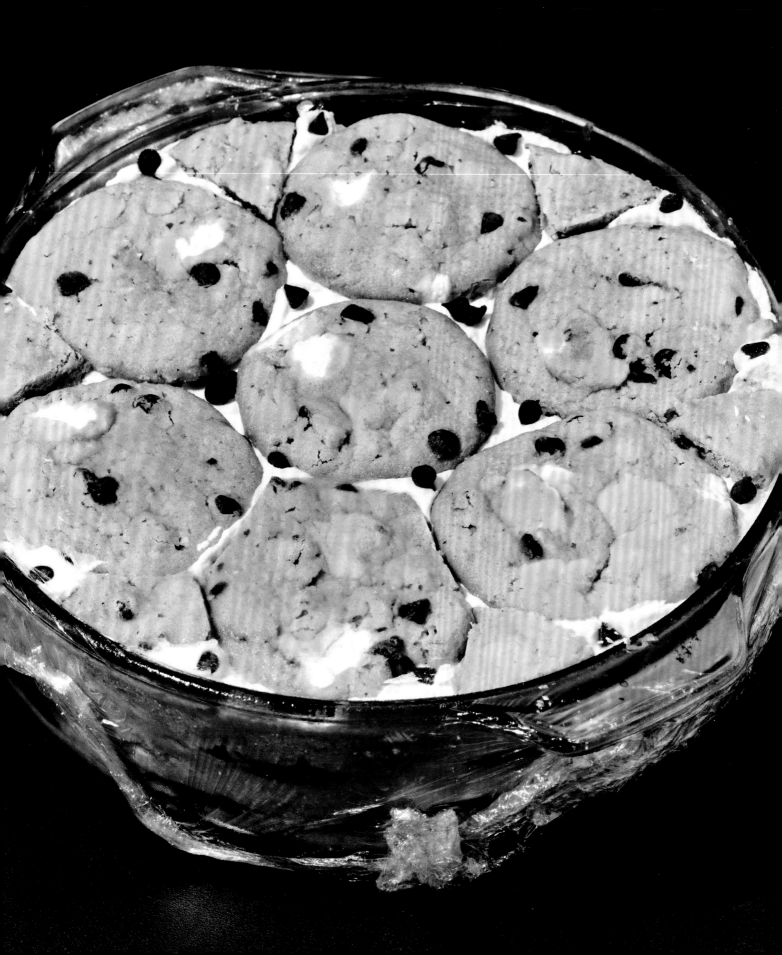

NO ONE'S MAD AT THAT (COOKIE HACKS)

GROWING UP, I FOUND MY ABILITY TO EXPRESS MYSELF through baking by walking the aisles of the grocery store. Bopping up and down, patient mom in tow, I was transfixed by the flavors, textures, and colors I found, each shelf bringing a world of possibility and inspiration. Returning to those aisles to inspire future generations of seven-year-olds (of all ages!) has been one of my biggest goals as we shape and grow Milk Bar. More than a decade in, and we achieved the full circle moment: proudly bringing our cookies to hundreds of grocery shelves across the country! Lifelong dreams realized and the unique thrill of seeing your world through the eyes of the next generation aside, this also means one amazing thing: I always have cookies in the pantry, ready and waiting for when creativity calls. Here are my "no one's mad at that" ways to get down with your fave store-bought cookies as a base.

ICE CREAM COOKIE CUPS

Makes 6

You would think that after years of baking and recipe developing, I would get used to doing dishes, but the truth is: I haven't. I will go to pretty elaborate lengths to avoid scrubbing and sudsing, which is what makes these individual cookie ice cream cups so brilliant in my book.

6 soft cookies

3 cups of your favorite ice cream

½ cup topping: nut butter, chocolate sauce, chocolate chips, sprinkles, jam

1. Pan-spray 6 cups of a muffin tin.

2. Smoosh 1 cookie into the base of each cup.

3. Top each cookie with a medium scoop of ice cream, smoothing to fill the cup. Dip a spoon in water to help manipulate the ice cream more easily. Leave a small divot in the top of each mound of ice cream. Fill the divot with a generous tablespoon of topping.

4. Place in the freezer to set—pop them out when you are ready to party.

ICEBOX COOKIE CAKE

Serves 8 to 12

There are some dishes from childhood that hold such power in our memories, you feel certain they must require loads of skill and tons of ingredients to make. Pigs in a blanket. Peanut butter balls, aka "buckeyes" in my household. Homemade mac 'n' cheese. Surely this deliciousness can't be easy? But oh, this fluffy, versatile showstopper of a cake sure is … but you should still take all the credit.

1 cup heavy cream

Flavor mix-in combos (options below)

16 to 24 cookies

1. In a stand mixer fitted with a whisk, whip the heavy cream until medium peaks form, about 4 minutes. Add your flavor mix-in combo and stir until well combined.

2. Cover a baking dish in a layer of cookies, filling edge to edge. Top the cookie layer with a layer of flavored whipped cream, adding fun bits like rainbow sprinkles or mini marshmallows.

3. Repeat until you get all the way to the top.

4. Refrigerate the brilliant mess for a minimum of 6 hours before digging in. The longer you let an ice box cake sit, the softer and more cake-like it will become. Serve out of the fridge or out of the freezer for even more ice cream vibes!

MIX-IN COMBOS

Compost
½ cup chocolate chips, melted, + ½ cup butterscotch chips, melted

Cornflake
1 cup chocolate chips, melted (or 1 cup fudge sauce, chocolate syrup, etc.) + 1 cup mini marshmallows or Marshmallow Fluff + ¼ cup Cornflake Crunch (page 159)

Confetti
1 tablespoon vanilla extract + ¼ cup rainbow sprinkles or 1 cup strawberry jam

COOKIE SHAKE WITH COOKIE SCOOP

Makes 1 shake

Listen, I'm not claiming to have invented milkshakes, but I am saying that I've made quite a few in my day and this formula never fails—that cookie sidecar slays every time.

→ I grew up in a waste-not, want-not household, and there was no use crying over broken cookies. Save your scraps and not so pretty pieces for shake o'clock.

3 cookies

2 scoops ice cream

1 long squeeze of flavored syrup or spoonful of jam

Splash of milk (optional, depending on how thick you like your shake)

1. In a blender, combine 2 of the cookies, the ice cream, and syrup or jam and mix on medium for 15 seconds or until smooth. Add milk if you want a thinner shake.

2. Serve in a tall glass with the final cookie on the side as a vehicle to dunk, scoop, and soak up all the shake-y goodness.

COOKIE TOAST

Makes 1 serving

Breakfast has never been my strong suit. For years my a.m. eating habits had mainly been strong black coffee and a tester compost cookie warm out of the oven as I crushed my prep list.

As I reach *cough* adulthood *cough*, I've tried to squeeze more sensibility into my diet by eating toast ... made from cookies.

→ If you use the Buttered Toast Cookie (page 247) as the base for your cookie toast, you are officially my hero.

2 cookies

2 spoonfuls of spreadable topping: jam, jelly, nut butter, Marshmallow Fluff, frosting

Handful of sprinkleable toppings: toasted nuts, Shortcake Crumbs (see page 114), granola, sprinkles, mini pretzels

1. Spread the flat side of each cookie with spreadable topping and evenly sprinkle with sprinkleable toppings.

2. Eat for breakfast, lunch, dinner, dessert, midnight snack—it's never a bad time for cookie toast.

BONUS RECIPE! THIS MILK BAR ALL-STAR SHOWS UP BIG wherever you add it—feel free to mix and match it in wherever your heart desires! Including on top of ice cream!

CORNFLAKE CRUNCH

Makes about 225g (3 cups)

130g	cornflakes	3¾ cups
36g	milk powder	⅓ cup + 1 T
30g	sugar	2 T + 1 tsp
3g	kosher salt	¾ tsp
100g	unsalted butter, melted	7 T

1. Heat the oven to 275°F. Pan-spray a half-sheet pan or line with parchment.

2. Pour the cornflakes into a medium bowl and crush them with your hands to one-quarter of their original size. Add the milk powder, sugar, and salt and toss to mix. Add the melted butter and toss to coat. As you toss, the butter will act as glue, binding the dry ingredients to the cereal and creating small clusters.

3. Spread the clusters onto the prepped sheet pan and bake at 275°F until the crunch looks toasted, smells buttery, and crunches gently when cooled slightly and chewed, 20 minutes.

4. Cool the cornflake crunch completely before storing or using in the Crunchy Cornflake Chocolate Chip Cookies recipe (see page 235). Stored in an airtight container at room temperature, the crunch will keep fresh for 1 week; in the fridge or freezer it will keep for 1 month.

Strawberry
Shortcake
Caramel Snaps
180

Candy Bar
Pie Snaps
167

Blueberry
Pie Snaps
185

Coffee
& Donut
Snaps
187

Grapefruit-
Ritz Snaps
169

Chocolate
Peppermint
Pretzel Snaps
177

Apple Cider
Donut Snaps
173

PB&J
Snaps
192

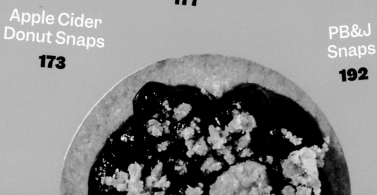

A FEW YEARS AGO, WE WERE BRAINSTORMING A BAKED GOOD WE
could make for the holiday season that could double as a great gift, a stocking stuffer, and a killer late-night splurge … you know, all the holiday essentials!

We knew it should have the handheld spirit of a cookie but have a candy/ chocolate vibe, too. To get those two ideas to come together, we started layering together textures and flavors: A cookie as a base. Then a flavorful center on top of it. Then something crunchy. Then all that encased in chocolate with a little teaser on top … oh, snap!

Once we landed on the formula for a snap, we blew it out. The possibilities for snaps are endless, but the recipes in this chapter are for my current top eight combos.

BUILDING A SNAP

Make snaps as fancy and fresh or as pantry-driven as you like, but here is the basic snap formula.

COOKIE BASE: Start with something thin and snappy, not too dense or thick. You want something substantial enough to be the foundation that holds all other layers on top without being a mouthful.

For example: A wafer or a thin cookie or a crispy, crunchy cookie. Heck, I'd even take a cracker.

FLAVOR CENTER: Top the cookie with something dense and sturdy, spreadable but not soupy. This is where a flavor story can really get going!

For example: You can really go anywhere with this, but for starters, how about peanut butter, Peppermint Pattie filling, nougat, Marshmallow Fluff, chewy caramel, dulce de leche, jam, or jelly?

CRUNCHY LAYER: Sprinkle on anything delicious that's small or that you can crumble into tiny, textural pieces to make a fun surprise hiding just below the surface.

For example: Mini pretzels, cereal, toffee bits, freeze-dried berries, crumbled space ice cream . . . you get the picture!

COATING: This is shell that keeps the fresh flavor story inside and the layers intact. Usually this is chocolate, but really you can use any item that's solid at room temperature but can melt down into a fluid state when warm. Sometimes we use a little oil to help with the viscosity.

For example: Dark chocolate, milk chocolate, white chocolate, butterscotch chips, peanut butter chips . . . you get the gist. And you can amp up flavor in any of the above with extract and color. Ka-pow.

TEASER: Finally, add a little flair on the outside that gives a sneak peek of what's to come.

For example: Chopped nuts, crushed candy canes, sprinkles, pretzel salt, strawberry drink mix, lemon peel . . . and now you're ready to start snapping!

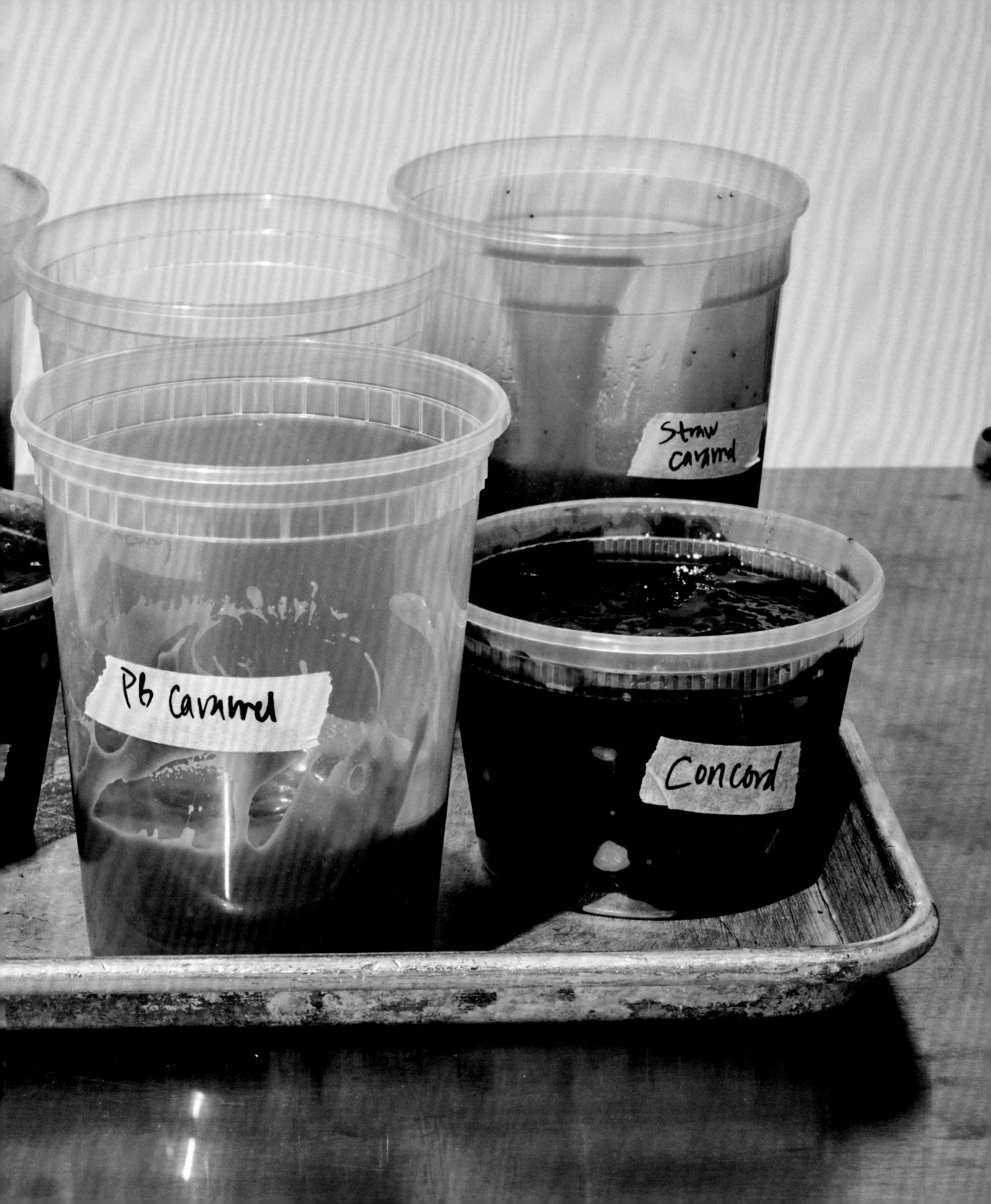
Straw caramel
Pb Caramel
Concord

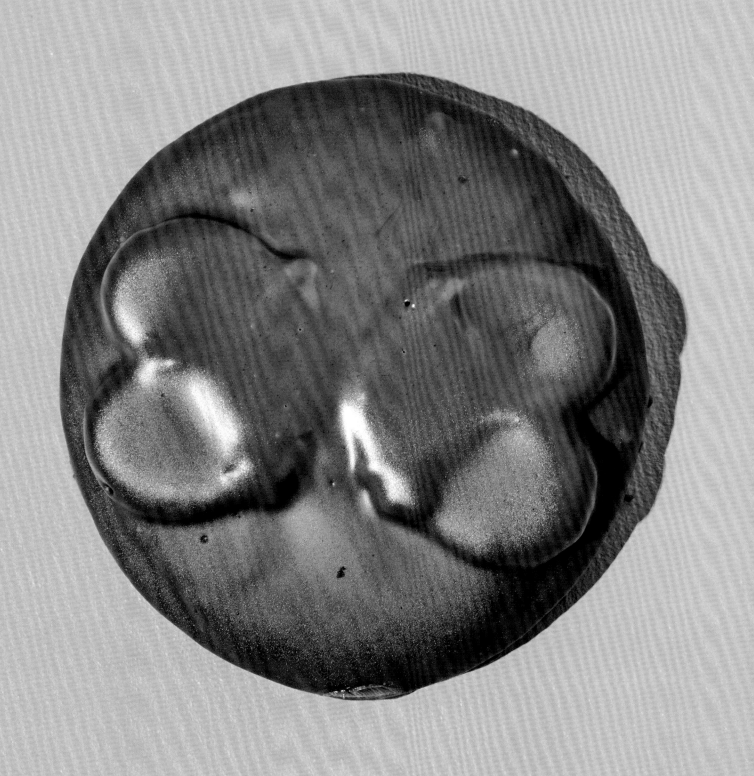

CANDY BAR PIE SNAPS

Makes twelve 3-inch round snaps

Thirteen-plus years ago when I opened the very first Milk Bar, my diet was two cornflake chocolate chip cookies hot out of the oven at approximately 6:12 a.m., several cups of coffee, and two slices of candy bar pie for dinner. I was literally fueled by sugar. And peanut butter. And chocolate. And caramel. So we made a pie out of those things, our homage to the Take 5 bar. That pie has long been semi-retired, but here we can resurrect one of the simplest, most salty-sweet, brilliant flavor combos in snap form.

→ Make the wafers and caramel a few hours in advance of making the chocolate coating and assembling the snaps.

1 recipe	Chocolate Wafers (page 179), cooled completely
¾ cup	Peanut Butter Caramel (recipe follows), cooled completely
24	mini pretzels
1 recipe	Vanilla Milk Chocolate Coating (recipe follows)

1. **Cookie Base & Flavor Center:** Top each wafer with 1 tablespoon of peanut butter caramel—don't get greedy! Using the back of your spoon, spread it evenly across the surface, but don't spread it all the way to the edge. You don't want it pouring over!

2. **Crunchy Layer:** Place 2 pretzels side by side on top of the caramel layer, pushing lightly so they stay in place. Transfer the wafers to a plate or baking sheet and pop them in the freezer to ensure maximum coolness while you set up your dipping and topping stations.

3. **Coating:** Put a large piece of parchment paper or a silicone baking mat on the counter, or pan-spray two sheet pans. Reheat the chocolate coating in the microwave in 15-second spurts to ensure it's warm and fluid. Repeat this warming process as needed if your coating cools down and thickens or forms lumps.

4. Pull the cookies out of the freezer and, one at a time, dunk each cookie, pretzel-side down, into the melted chocolate. Use a fork to flip the cookie right-side up to get an even coat.

5. Use the fork to scoop the cookie out of the chocolate. Tap the fork gently on the side of the bowl to encourage any excess chocolate to drip back into the chocolate mix and the outlines of the pretzel tops to show. Carefully transfer the dunked cookie to the parchment paper. Repeat until all the snaps are coated.

6. Allow the coated snaps to set for a minimum of 1 hour at room temp, or speed it up in the fridge or freezer.

7. Serve at room temperature. Snaps will keep in an airtight container in the fridge for up to 1 week or freezer for up to 1 month.

(recipe continues)

PEANUT BUTTER CARAMEL

Makes about 315g (1¼ cups)

→ If in doubt, strain the caramel to ensure that it's velvety smooth.

→ If in a hurry, refrigerate the caramel to cool and thicken completely.

200g	sugar	1 cup
140g	heavy cream	½ cup + 2 T
65g	peanut butter	¼ cup
8g	vanilla extract	2 tsp
2g	kosher salt	½ tsp

1. Make a dry caramel: In a heavy-bottomed medium saucepan, cook 50g (¼ cup) of the sugar over medium-high heat. As soon as the sugar starts to melt, use a heat-resistant spatula to move it constantly around the pan—you want it all to melt and caramelize evenly to a gorgeous amber color. Once the first amount of sugar has taken on color, add an additional 50g (¼ cup) of sugar to the existing caramel in the pan, repeating the previous steps—cook and stir, cook and stir, until the mixture is once again a gorgeous amber color. Continue adding 50g (¼ cup) sugar twice more until all the sugar has become one pretty pan of caramel.

2. Remove the saucepan from the heat. Very slowly and very carefully, stir in the heavy cream. The caramel will bubble up and steam; stand away until the steam dissipates. Use the heat-resistant spatula to stir the mixture together.

3. Carefully add the peanut butter, vanilla, and salt, stirring constantly. If the mixture is at all lumpy, put the saucepan back over medium heat and stir constantly until the sugar bits have dissolved and the mixture is smooth.

4. Let the caramel cool completely before using. It will keep in an airtight container in the fridge for up to 1 month.

VANILLA MILK CHOCOLATE COATING

Makes about 1 cup (enough to coat twelve 3-inch snaps)

340g	milk chocolate chips	12 oz (2 cups)
8g	canola oil	2 tsp
2g	vanilla extract	½ tsp

In a microwave-safe medium bowl, melt the milk chocolate chips and oil in the microwave in 30-second spurts, stirring after each, until smooth, about 2 minutes (but every microwave heats at different strengths). Use a heat-resistant spatula to ensure the mixture is fully melted and homogenous. Stir in the vanilla. Keep warm or remelt if necessary before using.

GRAPEFRUIT-RITZ SNAPS

Makes twelve 3-inch round snaps

I know it seems like a quirky flavor combo, but trust me, it's really a dynamic duo.

Back in the day, when my parents were my age, it was super hip to sit at your speckled breakfast table atop your linoleum-tiled floor, sprinkle a little salt over grapefruit halves, and eat the segments with a tiny serrated spoon. Salt and grapefruit work.

Then you balance that pucker with butter and sugar, and ta-da, grapefruit and Ritz crackers! They're a Batman-Robin-like combo in Milk Bar's flavor department—true superheroes who cannot be separated.

→ Make the wafers and grapefruit crème a few hours in advance of making the chocolate coating and assembling the snaps.

1 recipe	Caramelized Wafers (page 183), cooled completely	
¾ cup	Grapefruit Crème (recipe follows)	
12	Ritz crackers	
1 recipe	Grapefruit White Chocolate Coating (recipe follows)	
3g	grated grapefruit zest	1½ tsp

1. **Cookie Base & Flavor Center:** Top each wafer with 1 tablespoon of grapefruit crème—don't get greedy! Using the back of your spoon, spread it evenly across the surface, but don't spread it all the way to the edge. You don't want it pouring over!

2. **Crunchy Layer:** Place 1 Ritz cracker on top of each crème layer, pushing lightly so it stays in place. Transfer the wafers to a plate or baking sheet and pop them in the freezer to ensure maximum coolness while you set up your dipping and topping stations.

3. **Coating:** Put a large piece of parchment paper or a silicone baking mat on the counter or pan-spray 2 sheet pans. Reheat the chocolate coating in the microwave in 15-second spurts to ensure it's warm and fluid. Repeat this warming process as needed if your coating cools down and thickens or forms lumps.

4. Pull the cookies out of the freezer and, one at a time, dunk each cookie, cracker-side down, into the melted chocolate. Use a fork to flip the cookie right-side up to get an even coat.

5. Use the fork to scoop the cookie out of the chocolate. Tap the fork gently on the side of the bowl to encourage any excess chocolate to drip back into the chocolate mix. Carefully transfer the dunked cookie to the parchment paper.

6. **Teaser:** Sprinkle a little grapefruit zest over the surface of each. Repeat until all the snaps are coated and topped.

7. Allow the coated snaps to set for a minimum of 1 hour at room temperature, or speed it up in the fridge or freezer.

8. Serve at room temperature. The snaps will keep in an airtight container in the fridge for up to 1 week or freezer for up to 1 month.

(recipe continues)

GRAPEFRUIT CRÈME

Makes about 225g (1¼ cups)

→ We use shortening here to bring a luscious mouthfeel while amplifying the flavor of grapefruit. Butter has too much flavor and would steal the show!

→ Citric acid helps support the grapefruit pucker. Read up on it on page 14.

150g	confectioners' sugar	1¼ cups
45g	shortening	¼ cup
0.5g	kosher salt	⅛ tsp
0.25g	citric acid	pinch
35g	grapefruit juice	2 T + 1 tsp
3g	grated grapefruit zest	1½ tsp

1. In the bowl of a stand mixer fitted with the paddle attachment, cream together the confectioners' sugar, shortening, salt, and citric acid on medium for 1 minute until smooth. Scrape down the sides of the bowl with a spatula.

2. Add the grapefruit juice and zest, and mix on low speed about 1 minute until well combined.

3. Use immediately or keep in an airtight container in the fridge for up to 1 month.

GRAPEFRUIT WHITE CHOCOLATE COATING

Makes about 1 cup (enough to coat twelve 3-inch snaps)

340g	white chocolate chips	2 cups
8g	canola oil	2 tsp
6g	grated grapefruit zest	1 T (packed)
	red food coloring	4 drops
	yellow food coloring	2 drops

In a microwave-safe medium bowl, melt the white chocolate chips and oil in the microwave in 30-second spurts, stirring after each, until smooth, about 2 minutes (but every microwave heats at different strengths). Use a heat-resistant spatula to ensure the mixture is fully melted and homogenous. Stir in the grapefruit zest and food coloring until the mixture is an even, light pink-orange grapefruit color. Keep warm or remelt if necessary before using.

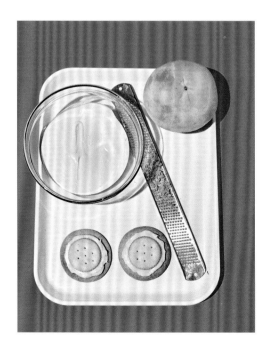

APPLE CIDER DONUT SNAPS

Makes twelve 3-inch round snaps

Every weekend from September to November, regardless of the weather or my geographic location, I want, nay, I NEED an apple cider donut. I just can't imagine fall without my weekly fix. When brainstorming for a fall snap at Milk Bar, I was the first to shout "Apple Cider Donut Snap!" (That was right after I screamed "Apple Cider Donut Cake! Apple Cider Donut Truffles!") Let's just say the team saw it coming. And, boy, did we knock it out of the park.

→ Make the wafers and caramel a few hours in advance of making the chocolate coating and assembling the snaps.

1 recipe	Cinnamon Donut Wafers (recipe follows), cooled completely		
¾ cup	Apple Cider Caramel (recipe follows), cooled completely		
14g	Cheerios cereal	120 pieces (about ½ cup)	
1 recipe	White Chocolate Coating (page 182)		
25g	turbinado sugar	2 T	
2g	ground cinnamon	½ tsp	

1. **Cookie Base & Flavor Center:** Top each wafer with 1 tablespoon of the caramel—don't get greedy! Using the back of your spoon, spread it evenly across the surface, but don't spread it all the way to the edge. (You don't want it pouring over!)

2. **Crunchy Layer:** Place about 10 Cheerios on top of the caramel layer, pushing lightly so they stay in place. Transfer the wafers to a plate or baking sheet and pop them in the freezer to ensure maximum coolness while you set up your dipping and topping stations.

3. **Coating:** Put a large piece of parchment paper or a silicone baking mat on the counter or pan-spray two sheet pans. Reheat the chocolate coating in the microwave in 15-second spurts to ensure it's warm and fluid. Repeat this warming process as needed if your coating cools down and thickens or forms lumps.

4. Pull the cookies out of the freezer and, one at a time, dunk each cookie, Cheerio-side down, into the melted chocolate. Use a fork to flip the cookie right-side up to get an even coat.

5. Use the fork to scoop the cookie out of the chocolate. Tap the fork gently on the side of the bowl to encourage any excess chocolate to drip back into the chocolate mix. Carefully transfer the dunked cookie to the parchment paper.

6. **Teaser:** Sprinkle the top of each cookie with ½ teaspoon of turbinado sugar and a pinch of ground cinnamon. Repeat until all the snaps are coated and topped.

7. Allow the coated snaps to set for a minimum of 1 hour at room temperature, or speed it up in the fridge or freezer.

8. Serve at room temperature. The snaps will keep in an airtight container in the fridge for up to 1 week or freezer for up to 1 month.

(recipe continues)

APPLE CIDER CARAMEL

Makes about 300g (1¼ cups)

→ If you can't get your hands on cider, use apple juice.

→ If in doubt, strain the caramel to ensure that it's velvety smooth.

→ If in a hurry, refrigerate the caramel to cool and thicken completely.

250g	sugar	1¼ cups
45g	heavy cream	3 T
80g	apple cider	⅓ cup
2g	kosher salt	½ tsp

1. Make a dry caramel: In a heavy-bottomed medium saucepan, cook 50g (¼ cup) of the sugar over medium-high heat. As soon as the sugar starts to melt, use a heat-resistant spatula to move it constantly around the pan—you want it all to melt and caramelize evenly to a gorgeous amber color. Once the first amount of sugar has taken on color, add an additional 50g (¼ cup) of sugar to the existing caramel in the pan, repeating the previous steps—cook and stir, cook and stir, until the mixture is once again a gorgeous amber color. Continue adding 50g (¼ cup) sugar at a time until all the sugar has become one pretty pan of caramel.

2. Remove the saucepan from the heat. Very slowly and very carefully, stir in the heavy cream. The caramel will bubble up and steam; stand away until the steam dissipates. Use the heat-resistant spatula to stir the mixture together.

3. Carefully add the apple cider and salt, stirring constantly. If the mixture is at all lumpy, put the saucepan back over medium heat and stir constantly until the sugar bits have dissolved and the mixture is smooth.

4. Let the caramel cool completely before using. It will keep in an airtight container in the fridge for up to 1 month.

UPCYCLED FRYER OIL

The key to making cookies taste like donuts is using oil that you've already used to fry something with. (Or asking a restaurant friend to bring you some oil from their fryer!) If you don't have fryer oil, go ahead and make your favorite recipe for one of following (or anything else you love that isn't too strongly flavored) and strain the oil afterward!

- Funnel cakes
- Corn dogs (or any other savory food in a thick, slightly sweet batter, though I wouldn't recommend fried chicken, etc.)
- Deep-fried cookies (à la county fair)
- Cannoli (we have a killer Bake Club recipe for this on milkbarstore.com)
- Donuts (to make donut cookies?! I would be so proud)
- Deep-fried, soft poached eggs (it's a thing, trust me)

CINNAMON DONUT WAFERS
Makes about twelve 3-inch rounds

Using fryer oil in this recipe is the key to making it taste like donuts (see Upcycled Fryer Oil, opposite), and it makes for a sandier-textured wafer, every bit as tasty as one bound together with butter.

→ Do not overmix the dough once you add flour—a great wafer is tender and snappy, which means minimal mixing!

→ I like to use a plastic pancake spatula or offset spatula to help transfer the dough rounds to the baking sheet and then again to get the baked wafers to release easily.

42g	unsalted butter, softened	3 T
70g	sugar	⅓ cup
70g	light brown sugar	⅓ cup (packed)
80g	upcycled fryer oil	⅓ cup
2g	vanilla extract	½ tsp
145g	flour	1 cup
2g	kosher salt	½ tsp
2g	ground cinnamon	½ tsp

1. In the bowl of a stand mixer fitted with the paddle attachment, cream together the butter, sugar, and brown sugar on medium speed about 1 minute until smooth. Scrape down the sides of the bowl with a spatula.

2. Add the oil and vanilla and paddle on low speed until well combined, about 1 minute. Scrape down the sides of the bowl with a spatula.

3. Add the flour, salt, and cinnamon and paddle on low speed until just combined, about 20 seconds.

4. Turn the dough out onto a work surface, divide in half, and flatten into 2 evenly shaped pancakes. Roll each dough pancake out between two sheets of parchment paper to a ½-inch thickness. (Using parchment here is a real sanity saver, so don't skip it!) Using a 3-inch round cookie cutter (or water glass), cut dough rounds as close to one another as possible. Refrigerate or freeze the entire sheet of dough for at least 30 minutes.

5. Heat the oven to 325°F. Pan-spray or line a sheet pan with parchment paper or a silicone baking mat.

6. Pop the chilled rounds off the parchment and transfer them to the prepared baking sheet, spacing them ¼ inch apart. (They don't spread in the oven!) Reshape the dough scraps into a ball and roll out anew, repeating until you run out of dough.

7. Bake each sheet of cookies at 325°F until the edges and center are a deep cinnamon donut color (color equals flavor here!), 12 to 15 minutes.

8. Let the rounds cool completely before layering into a snap. If made in advance, these cookies will last in an airtight container in the fridge for up to 5 days.

CHOCOLATE PEPPERMINT PRETZEL SNAPS

Makes twelve 3-inch snaps

This was the very first snap in Milk Bar history. It's the center of a Venn diagram between a slab of peppermint bark, a handful of Oreos, and a bag of pretzels. Though we only make these snaps during the holiday season, I've known many a Milk Bar hardbody and husband to stash extras come December and ration them all the way into the spring. Because they're dunked in chocolate, they stay fresh and delicious that long. That said, I personally don't understand how one is even built with that much self-control.

→ These minty babes call for peppermint extract, not mint extract. Mint extract has major toothpaste vibes; peppermint is candy cane mint, so stick with that one here.

→ Make the wafers and caramel a few hours in advance of making the chocolate coating and assembling the snaps.

1 recipe	Chocolate Wafers (recipe follows), cooled completely
¾ cup	Chewy Caramel (recipe follows), cooled completely
24	mini pretzels
1 recipe	Peppermint White Chocolate Coating (recipe follows)
20g	candy canes, crushed 2 T

1. **Cookie Base & Flavor Center:** Top each chocolate wafer with 1 tablespoon of caramel—don't get greedy! Using the back of your spoon, spread it evenly across the surface, but don't spread it all the way to the edge. You don't want it pouring over!

2. **Crunchy Layer:** Place 2 pretzels side by side on top of the caramel layer, pushing lightly so they stay in place. Transfer the wafers to a plate or baking sheet and pop them in the freezer to ensure maximum coolness while you set up your dipping and topping stations.

3. **Coating:** Put a large piece of parchment paper or a silicone baking mat on the counter or pan-spray two sheet pans. Reheat the chocolate coating in the microwave in 15-second spurts to ensure that it's warm and fluid. Repeat this warming process as needed during the following steps if your coating cools down and thickens or forms lumps.

4. Pull the cookies out of the freezer and, one at a time, dunk each cookie, pretzel-side down, into the melted chocolate. Use a fork to flip the cookie right-side up to get an even coat.

5. Use the fork to scoop the cookie out of the chocolate. Tap the fork gently on the side of the bowl to encourage any excess chocolate to drip back into the chocolate mix. Carefully transfer the dunked cookie to the parchment paper.

6. **Teaser:** Sprinkle the top of each cookie with ½ teaspoon crushed candy canes. Repeat until all the snaps are coated and topped.

7. Allow the coated snaps to set for a minimum of 1 hour at room temperature, or speed it up in the fridge or freezer.

8. Serve at room temperature. Snaps will keep in an airtight container in the fridge for up to 1 week or freezer for up to 1 month.

(recipe continues)

CHEWY CARAMEL

Makes about 300g (1¼ cups)

→ If in doubt, strain the caramel to ensure that it's velvety smooth.

→ If you're in a hurry, refrigerate the warm caramel to cool and thicken completely before using.

200g	sugar	1 cup
56g	unsalted butter	4 T
70g	heavy cream	⅓ cup
4g	vanilla extract	1 tsp
2g	kosher salt	½ tsp

1. Make a dry caramel: In a heavy-bottomed medium saucepan, cook 50g (¼ cup) of the sugar over medium-high heat. As soon as the sugar starts to melt, use a heat-resistant spatula to move it constantly around the pan—you want it all to melt and caramelize evenly to a gorgeous amber color. Once the first amount of sugar has taken on color, add an additional 50g (¼ cup) sugar to the existing caramel in the pan, repeating the previous steps—cook and stir, cook and stir, until the mixture is once again a gorgeous amber color. Continue adding 50g (¼ cup) sugar twice more until all your sugar has become one pretty pan of caramel.

2. Remove the saucepan from the heat. Very slowly and carefully, stir in the butter. The caramel will bubble up and steam; stand away until the steam dissipates. Use the heat-resistant spatula to stir the mixture together.

3. Carefully add the heavy cream, vanilla, and salt, stirring constantly. If the mixture is at all lumpy, put the saucepan back over medium heat and stir constantly until the sugar bits have dissolved and the mixture is smooth.

4. Let the caramel cool completely before using. It will keep in an airtight container in the fridge for up to 1 month.

PEPPERMINT WHITE CHOCOLATE COATING

Makes about 1 cup (enough to coat twelve 3-inch snaps)

340g	white chocolate chips	12 oz (2 cups)
8g	canola oil	2 tsp
1g	peppermint extract	¼ tsp

In a microwave-safe medium bowl, melt the white chocolate chips and oil in the microwave in 30-second spurts, stirring after each, until smooth, about 2 minutes (but every microwave heats at different strengths). Use a heat-resistant spatula to mix and ensure the mixture is fully melted and homogenous. Stir in the peppermint extract until well distributed. Keep warm or remelt if necessary before using.

CHOCOLATE WAFERS
Makes about twelve 3-inch rounds

→ The honey in this recipe gives the dough a pliability. If you don't have honey, feel free to sub in sugar, but know you'll have a slightly more brittle dough to work with.

→ Do not overmix the dough once you add flour—a great wafer is tender and snappy, which means minimal mixing!

→ Don't have a pro cookie cutter? Use a water glass (my go-to)!

→ I like to use a plastic pancake spatula or offset spatula to help transfer the dough rounds to the baking sheet and then again to get the baked wafers to release easily.

113g	unsalted butter, softened	1 stick (8 T)
100g	sugar	½ cup
90g	honey	¼ cup
2g	vanilla extract	½ tsp
145g	flour	1 cup
60g	cocoa powder	⅔ cup
2g	kosher salt	½ tsp
2g	baking soda	½ tsp

1. In the bowl of a stand mixer fitted with the paddle attachment, cream together the butter, sugar, honey, and vanilla on medium speed for 1 minute until smooth. Scrape down the sides of the bowl with a spatula.

2. Add the flour, cocoa powder, salt, and baking soda and paddle on low speed until just combined, about 20 seconds.

3. Turn the dough out onto a work surface, divide into 2 equal pieces, and flatten into 2 evenly shaped pancakes. Roll each dough pancake out between two sheets of parchment paper to a ½-inch thickness. (Using parchment here is a real sanity saver, so don't skip it!) Using a 3-inch round cookie cutter (or water glass), cut the dough rounds as close to one another as possible. Refrigerate or freeze the entire sheet of dough for at least 30 minutes.

4. Heat the oven to 325°F. Pan-spray or line two sheet pans with parchment paper or silicone baking mats.

5. Pop your chilled rounds off the parchment and transfer them to the prepared pans, spacing them ¼ inch apart. (They don't spread in the oven!) Reshape the dough scraps into a ball and roll out, cut, and chill, repeating until you run out of dough.

6. Bake each sheet of cookies at 325°F until the edges are set and the center is no longer glossy, 10 to 12 minutes. (It's hard to know when a chocolate wafer is baked properly, so set a timer!)

7. Let the wafers cool completely on the pan before layering into a snap. If made in advance, these cookies will last in an airtight container in the fridge for up to 5 days.

STRAWBERRY SHORTCAKE CARAMEL SNAPS

Makes twelve 3-inch round snaps

Mother's Day was upon us and we needed something fancy to wow all the moms of the world. Spring makes us think of strawberries, so we riffed on a strawberry shortcake, making caramelization the star. We put this together with a caramelized wafer (it's a killer cookie on its own or to support any other flavor!) and a strawberry caramel (yes, you can always sub out the liquid in a caramel with a fruit puree!), buttery shortbread, and freeze-dried strawberries. My mom, Greta, was DEFINITELY feeling like a queen after this one!

→ Make the wafers and caramel a few hours in advance of making the chocolate coating and assembling the snaps.

→ For the shortbread cookies, Pepperidge Farm Shortbread Cookies or Lorna Doones work great!

→ For the teaser, instead of freeze-dried strawberries, try ½ cup dried strawberries or 2 tablespoons strawberry drink mix or even pink sprinkles!

1 recipe	Caramelized Wafers (recipe follows), cooled completely
¾ cup	Chewy Strawberry Caramel (recipe follows), cooled completely
2 cups	crumbled shortbread cookies
1 recipe	White Chocolate Coating (recipe follows)
40g	freeze-dried strawberries, crushed ½ cup

1. **Cookie Base & Flavor Center:** Top each wafer round with 1 tablespoon of cooled caramel—don't get greedy! Using the back of your spoon, spread it evenly across the surface, but don't spread it all the way to the edge. You don't want it pouring over!

2. **Crunchy Layer:** Sprinkle a heaping 2 tablespoons of shortbread cookie pieces over each caramel layer, pushing lightly so they stay in place. Transfer the wafers to a plate or baking sheet and pop them in the freezer to ensure maximum coolness while you set up your dipping and topping stations.

3. **Coating:** Put a large piece of parchment paper or a silicone baking mat on the counter or pan-spray two sheet pans. Reheat the chocolate coating in the microwave in 15-second spurts to ensure it's warm and fluid. Repeat this warming process as needed during the following steps if your coating cools down and thickens or forms lumps.

4. Pull the cookies out of the freezer and, one at a time, dunk each cookie, caramel-side down, into the melted white chocolate. Use a fork to flip the cookie right-side up to get an even coat.

5. Use the fork to scoop the cookie out of the chocolate. Tap the fork gently on the side of the bowl to encourage any excess chocolate to drip back into the white chocolate mix. Carefully transfer the dunked cookie to the parchment paper.

6. **Teaser:** Sprinkle the top of each cookie with ½ teaspoon of the crushed freeze-dried strawberries. Repeat until all the snaps are coated and topped.

7. Allow the coated snaps to set for a minimum of 1 hour at room temperature, or speed it up in the fridge or freezer.

8. Serve at room temperature. Snaps will keep in an airtight container in the fridge for up to 1 week or freezer for up to 1 month.

(recipe continues)

CHEWY STRAWBERRY CARAMEL

Makes about 315g (1¼ cups)

→ If in doubt, strain the caramel to ensure that it's velvety smooth.

→ If in a hurry, refrigerate the caramel to cool and thicken completely.

→ Make the strawberry puree by blending and straining ¼ pound of fresh strawberries.

200g	sugar	1 cup
56g	unsalted butter	4 T
65g	strawberry puree	¼ cup
45g	heavy cream	3 T
1g	kosher salt	¼ tsp

1. Make a dry caramel: In a heavy-bottomed medium saucepan, heat 50g (¼ cup) of the sugar over medium-high heat. As soon as the sugar starts to melt, use a heat-resistant spatula to move it constantly around the pan—you want it all to melt and caramelize evenly to a gorgeous amber color. Once the first amount of sugar has taken on color, add an additional 50g (¼ cup) of sugar to the existing caramel in the pan, repeating the previous steps—cook and stir, cook and stir, until the mixture is once again a gorgeous amber color. Continue adding 50g (¼ cup) sugar twice more until all the sugar has become one pretty pan of caramel.

2. Remove the saucepan from the heat. Very slowly and very carefully, stir in the butter. The caramel will bubble up and steam; stand away until the steam dissipates. Use the heat-resistant spatula to stir the mixture together.

3. Carefully add the strawberry puree, heavy cream, and salt, stirring constantly. If the mixture is at all lumpy, put the saucepan back over medium heat and stir constantly until the sugar bits have dissolved and the mixture is smooth.

4. Let the caramel cool completely before using. It will keep in an airtight container in the fridge for up to 1 month.

WHITE CHOCOLATE COATING

Makes about 1 cup (enough to coat twelve 3-inch snaps)

340g	white chocolate chips	12 oz (2 cups)
8g	canola oil	2 tsp

In a microwave-safe medium bowl, melt the white chocolate chips and oil in the microwave in 30-second spurts, stirring after each, until smooth, about 2 minutes (but every microwave heats at different strengths). Use a heat-resistant spatula to ensure the mixture is fully melted and homogenous. Keep warm, or remelt if necessary before using.

CARAMELIZED WAFERS

Makes about twelve 3-inch rounds

→ Do not overmix the dough once you add flour—a great caramelized cookie round is tender and snappy, which means minimal mixing!

→ I like to use a plastic pancake spatula or offset spatula to help transfer the dough rounds to the baking sheet and then again to get the baked wafers to release easily.

113g	unsalted butter, softened	1 stick (8 T)
60g	light brown sugar	¼ cup (packed)
165g	flour	1 cup + 2 T
1g	kosher salt	¼ tsp

1. In the bowl of a stand mixer fitted with the paddle attachment, cream together the butter and brown sugar on medium speed for about 1 minute until smooth. Scrape down the sides of the bowl with a spatula.

2. Add the flour and salt and paddle on low speed until just combined, about 20 seconds.

3. Turn the dough out onto a work surface, divide into 2 equal pieces, and flatten into 2 evenly shaped pancakes. Roll each dough pancake out between two sheets of parchment paper to a ½-inch thickness. (Using parchment here is a real sanity saver, so don't skip it!) Using a 3-inch round cookie cutter (or water glass), cut the dough rounds as close to one another as possible. Refrigerate or freeze the entire sheet of dough for at least 30 minutes.

4. Heat the oven to 325°F. Pan-spray or line a sheet pan with parchment paper or a silicone baking mat.

5. Pop your chilled rounds off the parchment and transfer them to the prepared pan, spacing ¼ inch apart. (They don't spread in the oven!) Reshape the dough scraps into a ball and roll out, cut, and chill, repeating until you run out of dough.

6. Bake each pan of cookies at 325°F until the edges and roof of the cookie are a caramelized auburn brown, 10 to 12 minutes.

7. Let the wafers cool completely before layering into a snap. If made in advance, these cookies will last in an airtight container in the fridge for up to 5 days.

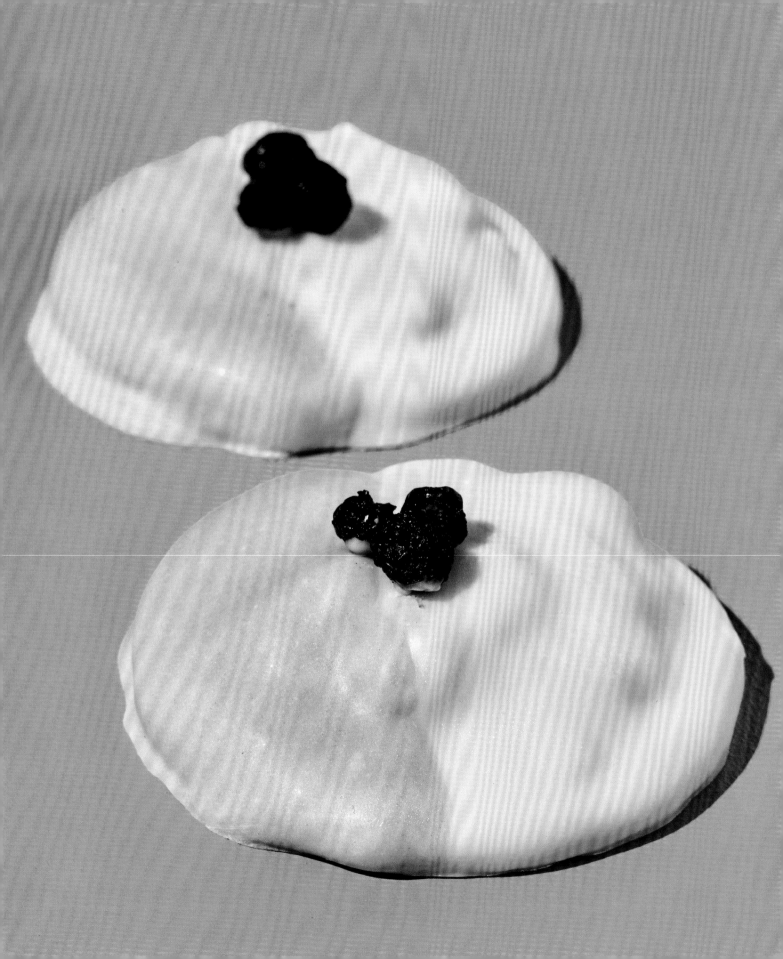

BLUEBERRY PIE SNAPS

Makes twelve 3-inch round snaps

I gotta be honest, I'm not really one to order a blueberry pie from a menu. No one makes it like my mom, who always mixes her blueberries with sour cream before baking so the tart berries have a sweet, creamy balance to them. These snaps are just like mom's pie, with a rich white chocolate exterior to lock in the big blueberry energy hiding inside, with flaky, butter pie wafers and crumbs fluttering in and out of bites. You may be ordering your pie by the snap rather than the slice sooner than you think!

→ Make the caramel, wafers, and jammy blueberries a few hours in advance of making the chocolate coating and assembling the snaps.

5 T	Chewy Caramel (page 178)
1 recipe	Pie Wafers & Crumbs (recipe follows), cooled completely
¾ cup	Jammy Blueberries (page 65), cooled completely
1 recipe	White Chocolate Coating (page 182)
20g	freeze-dried blueberries ½ cup

1. **Cookie Base & Flavor Center:** Fill a small zip-seal bag with the chewy caramel. Cut a small hole at one end and pipe a thin but tall ring of chewy caramel (about 1 teaspoon) just inside the edge of each pie wafer. Fill the center of each caramel-ringed wafer with 1 tablespoon of jammy blueberries—don't get greedy! Using the back of your spoon, spread it evenly across the surface, but don't spread it over the caramel. You don't want it pouring over!

2. **Crunchy Layer:** Sprinkle 1 teaspoon of pie wafer crumbs on top of each blueberry layer, pushing lightly so they stay in place. Transfer the cookies to a plate or baking sheet and pop them in the freezer to ensure maximum coolness while you set up your dipping and topping stations.

3. **Coating:** Put a large piece of parchment paper or a silicone baking mat on the counter, or pan-spray two sheet pans. Reheat the chocolate coating in the microwave in 15-second spurts to ensure that it's warm and fluid. Repeat this warming process as needed if your coating cools down and thickens or forms lumps.

4. Pull the cookies out of the freezer and, one at a time, dunk each cookie, crumb-side down, into the melted chocolate. Use a fork to flip the cookie right-side up to get an even coat.

5. Use the fork to scoop the cookie out of the chocolate. Tap the fork gently on the side of the bowl to encourage any excess chocolate to drip back into the chocolate mix. Carefully transfer the dunked cookie to the parchment paper.

6. **Teaser:** Sprinkle the top of each cookie with a few freeze-dried blueberries. (If you have any white chocolate left, you can color it light blue and do a second little dunk like in the pics!) Repeat until all the snaps are coated and topped.

7. Allow the coated snaps to set for a minimum of 1 hour at room temperature, or speed it up in the fridge or freezer.

8. Serve at room temperature. The snaps will keep in an airtight container in the fridge for up to 1 week or freezer for up to 1 month.

(recipe continues)

PIE WAFERS & CRUMBS

Makes about twelve 3-inch rounds + ¼ cup crumbs

→ Do not overmix the dough once you add flour—a great wafer is tender and snappy, which means minimal mixing!

→ I like to use a plastic pancake spatula or offset spatula to help transfer the dough rounds to the baking sheet and then again to get the baked wafers to release easily.

140g	unsalted butter, softened	10 T
70g	sugar	⅓ cup
1	large egg yolk	
15g	water	1 T
235g	flour	1½ cups + 1 T
4g	kosher salt	1 tsp

1. In the bowl of a stand mixer fitted with the paddle attachment, cream together the butter and sugar on medium speed for about 1 minute until smooth. Scrape down the sides of the bowl with a spatula.

2. Add the egg yolk and water and mix on low speed for 1 minute until well combined. Scrape down the sides of the bowl with a spatula.

3. Add the flour and salt and paddle on low speed just until combined, about 20 seconds.

4. Turn the dough out onto a work surface, divide in half, and flatten into 2 evenly shaped pancakes. Roll each dough pancake out between two sheets of parchment paper to a ½-inch thickness. (Using parchment here is a real sanity saver, so don't skip it!) Using a 3-inch round cookie cutter (or water glass), cut the dough rounds as close to one another as possible. Refrigerate or freeze the entire sheet of dough for at least 30 minutes.

5. Heat the oven to 325°F. Pan-spray or line two sheet pans with parchment paper or silicone baking mats.

6. Pop your chilled rounds off the parchment and transfer them to one of the prepared pans, spacing them ¼ inch apart. (They don't spread in the oven!) Reshape the dough scraps into a ball, roll out, cut, and chill, repeating to get 12 cookies.

7. Once you have 12 rounds cut, take the remaining dough and break it up in your hands to form small clusters the size of peas. Spread them out evenly on the second sheet pan.

8. Bake the crumbs at 325°F until they have a very deep golden brown color, 10 to 12 minutes. Bake the wafers 3 to 5 minutes longer than the crumbs, 15 to 17 minutes total, until the wafers are a very deep golden brown color as well. (It takes the wafers longer than you think to achieve this, but it is crucial to the pie flavor coming to life.)

9. Let the crumbs and wafers cool completely before layering into a snap. If made in advance, these crumbs and cookies will last in airtight containers in the fridge for up to 5 days.

COFFEE & DONUT SNAPS

Makes twelve 3-inch round snaps

Call me a sucker for indulging in a classic food-and-drink-pairing flavor story, but the outcome is far from ordinary. Coffee fudge brings a mocha moment, Cheerios bring the crunch, the caramel chocolate coating brings a surprise wow, and all that gets wrapped up into one snappy donut bite. In my dreams, I've already opened a Donut Snap Shop chain.

→ Make the wafers and fudge a few hours in advance of making the chocolate coating and assembling the snaps.

→ For a different textural vibe, sub in mini marshmallows (90g/1¾ cups) for the Cheerios.

1 recipe	Donut Wafers (recipe follows), cooled completely	
¾ cup	Coffee Fudge (recipe follows), cooled completely	
14g	Cheerios cereal	120 pieces (about ½ cup)
1 recipe	Caramel Chocolate Coating (recipe follows)	
8g	instant coffee	2 T

1. **Cookie Base & Flavor Center:** Top each wafer with 1 tablespoon of the fudge—don't get greedy! Using the back of your spoon, spread it evenly across the surface, but don't spread it all the way to the edge. You don't want it pouring over!

2. **Crunchy Layer:** Place about 10 Cheerios on top of each fudge layer, pushing lightly so they stay in place. Transfer the wafers to a plate or baking sheet and pop them in the freezer to ensure maximum coolness while you set up your dipping and topping stations.

3. **Coating:** Put a large piece of parchment paper or a silicone baking mat on the counter or pan-spray two sheet pans. Reheat the chocolate coating in the microwave in 15-second spurts to ensure it's warm and fluid. Repeat this warming process as needed if your coating cools down and thickens or forms lumps.

4. Pull the cookies out of the freezer and, one at a time, dunk each cookie, Cheerio-side down, into the melted chocolate. Use a fork to flip the cookie right-side up to get an even coat.

5. Use the fork to scoop the cookie out of the chocolate. Tap the fork gently on the side of the bowl to encourage any excess chocolate to drip back into the chocolate mix. Carefully transfer the dunked cookie to the parchment paper.

6. **Teaser:** Sprinkle the top of each cookie with ½ teaspoon of instant coffee. Repeat until each cookie is coated and topped.

7. Allow the coated snaps to set for a minimum of 1 hour at room temperature, or speed it up in the fridge or freezer. Serve at room temperature. The snaps will keep in an airtight container in the fridge for up to 1 week or freezer for up to 1 month.

(recipe continues)

CARAMEL CHOCOLATE COATING

Makes about 1 cup (enough to coat twelve 3-inch snaps)

→ Dulcey is a caramelized white chocolate coating made by Valrhona. It's EPIC, especially in this snap. Take to the Internet to get your hands on it. If you really don't want to go the distance (I'll be a little sad, but I'll get over it), follow the recipe for White Chocolate Coating (page 182) with any chocolate (white, milk, or dark). Dulcey does not need any additional oil like the other coatings because it has enough cocoa butter in its formula to stay fluid and thin in its melted phase to coat the snaps.

340g	Dulcey	12 oz

In a microwave-safe medium bowl, melt the Dulcey in the microwave in 30-second spurts , stirring after each, until smooth, about 1½ minutes (but every microwave heats at different strengths). Use a heat-resistant spatula to ensure the mixture is fully melted and homogenous. Keep warm, or remelt if necessary before using.

COFFEE FUDGE

Makes about 315g (1¼ cups)

→ The cream of tartar helps bridge the chocolate and coffee and softens the acidic notes. It also helps keep the fudge super glossy.

→ If in doubt, strain your fudge to ensure that it's velvety smooth, and if you're in a hurry, refrigerate the fudge to cool and thicken it completely.

140g	sugar	⅔ cup
110g	heavy cream	½ cup
4g	vanilla extract	1 tsp
84g	semisweet chocolate chips	3 oz (⅓ cup)
20g	cocoa powder	¼ cup
9g	instant coffee	2 T + 1 tsp
2g	kosher salt	½ tsp
0.5g	cream of tartar	pinch

1. In a heavy-bottomed medium saucepan, combine the sugar, heavy cream, and vanilla and bring to a boil over medium-high heat.

2. In a heatproof bowl, combine the chocolate, cocoa powder, instant coffee, salt, and cream of tartar. Pour the saucepan's hot contents into the bowl and let sit for 30 seconds.

3. Whisk all ingredients together until smooth. If the mixture is at all lumpy, put the entire mixture back in the saucepan over medium heat and stir constantly until smooth.

4. Let the fudge cool completely before using. It will keep in an airtight container in the fridge for up to 1 month.

(recipe continues)

DONUT WAFERS

Makes about twelve 3-inch rounds

→ Do not overmix the dough once you add flour—a great wafer is tender and snappy, which means minimal mixing!

→ I like to use a plastic pancake spatula or offset spatula to help transfer the dough rounds to the baking sheet and then again to get the baked wafers to release easily.

→ Read up on Upcycled Fryer Oil on page 174.

42g	unsalted butter, softened	3 T
70g	sugar	⅓ cup
70g	light brown sugar	⅓ cup (packed)
80g	upcycled fryer oil	⅓ cup
2g	vanilla extract	½ tsp
145g	flour	1 cup
2g	kosher salt	½ tsp

1. In the bowl of a stand mixer fitted with the paddle attachment, cream together the butter, sugar, and brown sugar on medium speed until smooth, about 1 minute. Scrape down the sides of the bowl with a spatula.

2. Add the oil and vanilla and paddle on low speed until well combined, about 1 minute. Scrape down the sides of the bowl with a spatula.

3. Add the flour and salt and paddle on low speed until just combined, about 20 seconds.

4. Turn the dough out onto a work surface, divide in half, and flatten into 2 evenly shaped pancakes. Roll each dough pancake out between two sheets of parchment paper to a ½-inch thickness. (Using parchment here is a real sanity saver, so don't skip it!) Using a 3-inch round cookie cutter (or water glass), cut the dough rounds as close to one another as possible. Refrigerate or freeze the entire sheet of dough for at least 30 minutes.

5. Heat the oven to 325°F. Pan-spray or line a sheet pan with parchment paper or a silicone baking mat.

6. Pop the chilled rounds off the parchment and transfer them to the prepared pan, spacing them ¼ inch apart. (They don't spread in the oven!) Reshape the dough scraps into a ball and roll out anew, repeating until you run out of dough.

7. Bake each sheet of cookies at 325°F until the edges and center are a golden brown donut color, 12 to 15 minutes.

8. Let the wafers cool completely before layering into a snap. If made in advance, these cookies will last in an airtight container in the fridge for up to 5 days.

PB&J SNAPS

Makes twelve 3-inch round snaps

Growing up, my go-to sammie was a cheese sandwich with mustard, sometimes Cool Ranch Doritos snuck in. If Greta packed these cookies in my lunch bag every day, I have a feeling things might have turned out differently for me. But as it was, I was never really into PB&J, until I discovered my love for this flavor combo decades later and am still rocking out. This is the only snap that does not have a sandy/textural layer between the smooth/chewy layer and the chocolate coating. This is because the crunchy peanuts will get soggy in the jelly, so we put them on the outside.

→ I like to take a little bit of my white chocolate and dye it purple (1 drop red, 1 drop blue food coloring) and drizzle it on using a zip-seal bag with a small hole cut out. It's an extra step, but I think it makes it look very nice. You do you.

→ Make the wafers and jelly a few hours in advance of making the chocolate coating and assembling the snaps.

1 recipe	PB Wafers (opposite), cooled completely
1 recipe	Jellied Jelly (recipe follows), cooled completely
1 recipe	White Chocolate Coating (page 182)
75g	salted roasted peanuts, ½ cup chopped

1. **Cookie Base & Flavor Center:** Top each wafer with 1 tablespoon of jelly—don't get greedy! Using the back of your spoon, spread it evenly across the surface, but don't spread it all the way to the edge. You don't want it pouring over!

2. Transfer the wafers to a plate or baking sheet and pop them in the freezer to ensure maximum coolness while you set up your dipping and topping stations.

3. **Coating:** Put a large piece of parchment paper or a silicone baking mat on the counter or pan-spray two sheet pans. Reheat the chocolate coating in the microwave in 15-second spurts to ensure it's warm and fluid. Repeat this warming process as needed if your coating cools down and thickens or forms lumps.

4. Pull the cookies out of the freezer and, one at a time, dunk each cookie, jelly-side down, into the melted chocolate. Use a fork to flip the cookie right-side up to get an even coat.

5. Use the fork to scoop the cookie out of the chocolate. Tap the fork gently on the side of the bowl to encourage any excess chocolate to drip back into the chocolate mix. Carefully transfer the dunked cookie to the parchment paper.

6. **Teaser:** Sprinkle the top of each cookie with 2 teaspoons of chopped roasted peanuts. Repeat until all the snaps are coated and topped.

7. Allow the coated snaps to set for a minimum of 1 hour at room temperature, or speed it up in the fridge or freezer.

8. Serve at room temperature. The snaps will keep in an airtight container in the fridge for up to 1 week or freezer for up to 1 month.

PB WAFERS

Makes about twelve 3-inch rounds

This wafer is more sandy than others, due to the epically nutty ratio of peanut butter to butter. As such, this dough will be firmer and drier than the other wafer doughs. Don't fret, it's simply because of the difference in fats. One bite of this wafer and you may never make it to snap town.

→ Do not overmix the dough once you add flour—a great wafer is tender and snappy, which means minimal mixing!

→ I like to use a plastic pancake spatula or offset spatula to help transfer the dough rounds to the baking sheet and then again to get the baked wafers to release easily.

195g	creamy peanut butter	¾ cup
56g	unsalted butter, softened	4 T
140g	sugar	⅔ cup
1	large egg yolk	
3g	vanilla extract	¾ tsp
110g	flour	¾ cup
2g	kosher salt	½ tsp
1g	baking soda	¼ tsp

1. In a stand mixer fitted with the paddle attachment, combine the peanut butter and butter, and paddle on medium speed for about 1 minute until smooth. Scrape down the sides of the bowl with a spatula.

2. Add the sugar and paddle on medium speed until combined, about 20 seconds. Scrape down the sides of the bowl with a spatula.

3. Add the egg yolk and vanilla and paddle on low speed about 1 minute until well combined. Scrape down the sides of the bowl with a spatula.

4. Add the flour, salt, and baking soda and paddle on low speed until just combined, about 20 seconds.

5. Turn the dough out onto a work surface, divide in half, and flatten into 2 evenly shaped pancakes. Roll each dough pancake out between two sheets of parchment paper to a ½-inch thickness. (Using parchment here is a real sanity saver, so don't skip it!) Using a 3-inch round cookie cutter (or water glass), cut dough rounds as close to one another as possible. Refrigerate or freeze the entire sheet of dough for at least 30 minutes.

6. Heat the oven to 325°F. Pan-spray or line a sheet pan with parchment paper or a silicone baking mat.

7. Pop your chilled rounds off the parchment and transfer them to the prepared pan, spacing them ¼ inch apart. (They don't spread in the oven!) Reshape the dough scraps into a ball, roll out, cut, and chill, repeating until you run out of dough.

8. Bake each sheet of cookies at 325°F until the edges and the center are a rich auburn brown and your kitchen smells like a nutty paradise, about 15 minutes.

9. Let the wafers cool completely before layering into a snap. If made in advance, these cookies will last in an airtight container in the fridge for up to 5 days.

(recipe continues)

JELLIED JELLY

Makes about 308g (1 cup)

Cooking down the jelly makes the flavor more concentrated.

→ I'm a grape jelly gal, but if you prefer strawberry jam or raspberry preserves, feel free to sub in here.

575g	Concord grape jelly	1½ cups

1. In a heavy-bottomed medium saucepan, bring the jelly to a boil over medium-high heat. Reduce the temperature to a simmer and cook until the jelly reduces by one-third, about 20 minutes, stirring every few minutes with a heat-resistant spatula to ensure even heat distribution.

2. Remove the saucepan from the heat. Let the jelly cool completely before using. It will keep in an airtight container in the fridge for up to 1 month.

COOKIES THAT LIKE TO PARTY

AS MUCH AS I ADMIRE COOKIES FOR THEIR PLACE IN THE EVERYDAY, they also party just as well as any cake or pie I know…if not better.

Some reasons why cookies are your party-planning best friend:

1. No cutlery required means fewer dishes.
2. They aren't as much of a commitment as a slice of cake, meaning you can try more varieties.
3. Wrapping up leftovers is a breeze, and everyone says yes to extra cookies for the road.
4. They make your house smell incredible!

When it comes to picking cookies for a bash, I like to go big and bold. Making your dough into one giant Honey-I-Shrunk-the-Kids-style cookie cake is a crowd pleaser, as is layering on colorful coats of icing and sprinkles. And don't sleep on the power of graham crackers layered up with banana and buttery peanut butter to woo a crowd. This chapter is full of all different kinds of cookies: Some are fancy, some are XL—but they all like to party!

GLAZED TRIANGLES

Makes 16 cookies

These colorful triangles are what the outside of a Pop-Tart wants to grow up to be. Flaky and rich with a pure-at-heart glaze on top, they are proof that the simple things in life are oftentimes the best. If you want to double up your layers and spread some Jammy Blueberries (page 65) in between, live it up, my friend!

Impossibly light and flaky, these are made with a version of puff pastry called a "quick puff." They combine butter and flour together so that when they bake in the oven, the tiny amount of water in those butter pieces steam and puff the dough up, leaving behind magical little layers as thin as paper.

→ If you're in a hurry or aren't ready to take on the quick puff pastry, I absolutely give you permission to use store-bought frozen puff pastry here. Defrost a sheet on a clean countertop at room temperature for 20 to 30 minutes until pliable, shape your pastry into two 12 × 4-inch rectangles, then pick up at step 9.

225g	flour	1½ cups + 1 T + extra for dusting
140g	unsalted butter, cut into cubes	10 T
4g	kosher salt	1 tsp
80g	water	⅓ cup
1 recipe	Strawberry Glaze (recipe follows) or Lemon Glaze (recipe follows)	
12g	sprinkles	1 T

1. Combine the flour, butter cubes, and salt in a bowl and chill in the freezer for 20 minutes.

2. Pour the water into a cup with several ice cubes and set aside to chill.

3. Use masking tape to tape a large piece of parchment down to your work surface. Break up the butter cubes into the flour and toss to coat. Tip it out onto the rolling surface.

4. Use a rolling pin to press down firmly on the butter cubes to flatten them into the flour. As they flatten, begin to roll and extend them into the flour. It will be hard and awkward at first, but they will begin to yield after a few rolls. Use your palm to flatten any pesky pieces as necessary.

5. When the cubes become flakes, gather the mixture into a pile and drizzle 40g (scant 3 tablespoons) of the cold water (no ice!) over the top and use a fork to quickly toss and scatter it evenly throughout the mixture. Repeat with another 40g (scant 3 tablespoons) water. The dusty flour should begin to transform into larger, curd-like bits of dough.

6. Still on the parchment surface, gather the mixture into a rough square and begin to roll it out, using a light dusting of flour on top or on bottom, extending it into a 12 × 6-inch rectangle. Fold the dough into thirds like a letter to make a 4 × 6-inch rectangle. Turn the seam of the letter-folded dough to the right, and roll out, dusting with flour and folding into thirds again. Repeat for the third time. At this point you should have a cohesive dough, with butter incorporated and marbled throughout.

7. Wrap the dough in plastic and chill in the fridge for 30 minutes.

8. Heat the oven to 400°F. Pan-spray or line a half-sheet pan with parchment paper or a silicone baking mat.

9. On a clean countertop, divide the dough in half and roll each piece out to a 12 × 4-inch rectangle,

(recipe continues)

lightly dusting the countertop or surface of the dough as needed and place side-by-side on the prepared pan. Cover and freeze for 10 minutes, until firm.

10. Use a knife or pizza cutter to trim each edge of the pastry rectangle to form sharp, clean edges. With a fork, dock (poke holes) up and down each piece of pastry 30 times, side to side, end to end. These holes help the pastry bake uniformly and avoid irregular puffing.

11. Bake the pastry rectangles at 400°F until puffed, baked through, and deeply golden, 18 to 22 minutes.

12. Let the pastry cool for 5 minutes on the pan, then very carefully transfer to a large cutting board.

13. Generously drip half the glaze over the surface of the pastry and use an offset spatula or the back of a dinner spoon to smooth and spread, leaving an ⅛-inch border around the edges. Scatter with sprinkles and repeat with the second piece. Let the glaze set until it forms a skin and is dry to the touch, 10 to 15 minutes.

14. With the long side of the pastry rectangle facing you, cut across and back again, forming triangles that are 1½ inches wide at the base and 4 inches tall. You will get eight delightful triangles per pastry rectangle.

15. Transfer the cookies to a plate or an airtight container for storage. At room temperature, the cookies will keep fresh for 3 days.

STRAWBERRY GLAZE
Makes about 1 cup

240g	confectioners' sugar	2 cups
14g	lemon juice	1 T
15g	water	1 T
25g	strawberry jam	1 T + 1 tsp
1g	kosher salt	¼ tsp

In a medium bowl, whisk together the confectioners' sugar, lemon juice, water, strawberry jam, and salt until smooth. Cover until ready to use.

LEMON GLAZE
Makes about 1 cup

240g	confectioners' sugar	2 cups
50g	lemon juice	3 T + 1 tsp
1g	kosher salt	¼ tsp
	yellow food coloring	2 drops

In a medium bowl, whisk together the confectioners' sugar, lemon juice, salt, and food coloring until smooth. Cover until ready to use.

PUFF & JAM FLOWERS

Makes 9 cookies

These are a hard cookie to categorize, but essentially they're a pastry cookie, a toast and jam affair but in handheld, crunchy, flaky, buttery, jammy form. Did your brain just explode?

The best part is that they are a complete breeze to make. If you haven't already been converted to a store-bought puff pastry, now is the time, my friend. I keep a log of puff pastry in the freezer from time to time when I want to feel fancy but only have 15 minutes. #NoShame

→ If you're not feeling the store-bought puff pastry, swap in half of the dough from the Glazed Triangles (page 200), roll into a 9 x 9-inch square, and start at step 2.

→ The thicker (less runny) the jam, the better here!

	frozen puff pastry	1 sheet (7 or 8 oz)
1	large egg	
	kosher salt	pinch
64g	thick strawberry jam (or your favorite!)	3 T
25g	turbinado sugar	2 T

1. On a clean countertop, unroll and thaw the sheet of puff pastry at room temperature for 20 to 30 minutes until pliable.

2. Heat the oven to 375°F. Pan-spray or line a half-sheet pan with parchment paper or a silicone baking mat.

3. Score then cut the puff pastry into nine 3 × 3-inch squares.

4. Beat the egg with a pinch of salt and lightly brush the edges of each pastry square with egg wash. Top each square with 1 teaspoon of jam, leaving the egg-washed edges bare.

5. Lift the 4 corners of each pastry square to the center and pinch together to secure. Repeat once more with the newly formed corners to form a little package filled with jam. Flatten gently with your palm to form a puck.

6. Arrange the jam pucks on the prepared pan seam-side down. Freeze for 10 minutes.

7. Use a paring knife to make 8 evenly spaced cuts around each cookie. The cuts should nearly meet in the center but leave a small center margin intact, like the hub of a wheel.

8. Pick up and twist each petal once to the right so the exposed side is now facing up. If a lot of jam leaks onto the pan in this process, you may have cut too close to the center, but not to worry, simply replace the bottom parchment so it doesn't scorch in the oven.

9. Brush the flowers with egg wash and sprinkle turbinado sugar in each cookie's center.

10. Bake at 375°F until puffed and deep golden, 16 to 18 minutes.

11. Serve warm or cool completely on the pan. Transfer the cookies to a plate or an airtight container for storage. At room temperature, the cookies will keep fresh for 2 days; in the freezer, they will keep for 1 month.

Gingerbread Toffee

GINGERBREAD TOFFEE SQUARES

Makes 24 squares

My holiday inner dialogue is often: "I'd like ten baked goods as my sustenance today." I wait all year long to go overboard on dessert for a solid month and a half. The best part of these flaky, burnt sugar squares is that they satisfy the whole holiday baked good/sustenance thing, but they also help round out the offering with the spice and warmth of gingerbread. When I eat too many cut-out cookies, instead of drinking a cup of ginger tea to settle the tummy, I just tuck into a square of these. They will also be the sleeper star at any holiday cookie party/cookie swap (page 87).

→ This recipe is killer with saltine crackers, but graham crackers, butter crackers, or any other square or rectangular crackers or cookie you have on hand would work great. Bonus points if you use actual gingerbread!

→ In this batch I call for molasses, cinnamon, and ginger, but feel free to sub in other syrups or spices you're feeling to the mix: maple, honey, turmeric, coriander, pumpkin pie spice blend, nutmeg, or go all cinnamon, etc.

160g	saltine crackers	(about 40 crackers)
168g	unsalted butter	1½ sticks (12 T)
170g	light brown sugar	¾ cup (packed)
85g	molasses	¼ cup
5g	kosher salt	1¼ tsp
3.5g	ground ginger	1¾ tsp
2.75g	ground cinnamon	1¼ tsp
	White chocolate chips, melted, for decoration	
	Colored sugar sprinkles or nonpareils, for decoration	

1. Heat the oven to 350°F. Pan-spray a 9 × 13-inch baking dish.

2. In a single layer, line the baking dish with crackers, breaking crackers as necessary to fill the entire dish.

3. In a medium saucepan, combine the butter, brown sugar, molasses, salt, ginger, and cinnamon and bring to a boil over medium heat. Simmer on low heat for 3 minutes and remove from the stovetop.

4. Pour the delicious-smelling spice mixture evenly over the cracker layer.

5. Transfer to the oven and bake at 350°F until it bubbles, caramelizes, and infiltrates the cracker layer with gingerbread magic, about 10 minutes.

6. Cool completely, then decorate with melted white chocolate chip swirls and colorful sprinkles. Break into 24 square-ish pieces. Store in an airtight container at room temperature for up to 3 days.

PB BANANA SQUARES

Makes 24 squares

Sometimes the heart wants what it wants. Like little layered PB&B dessert sandwiches, these squares could not be easier, they are endlessly flexible, and they come together with the shortest list of ingredients, yet I find myself thinking of them constantly. Perfect for a potluck party that needs a tasty dessert for a crowd, throw these together when company calls or a craving strikes, and let your heart (and belly) be as happy as mine.

→ This recipe is killer with graham crackers, but saltines, butter crackers, or any other square or rectangular crackers you have on hand would work great.

→ In this batch I call for peanut butter and banana—if the flavor combo ain't broke don't fix it—but feel free to sub in other vibes you're feeling to the mix: almond butter, Nutella, Marshmallow Fluff, raspberry jam, apple slices, coconut, chocolate... get wild.

250g	graham crackers	18 crackers (2 sleeves)
3	bananas, sliced into ¼-inch pieces	
168g	unsalted butter	1½ sticks (12 T)
170g	light brown sugar	¾ cup (packed)
260g	peanut butter	1 cup
4g	vanilla extract	1 tsp
5g	kosher salt	1¼ tsp

1. Heat the oven to 325°F. Pan-spray a 9 × 13-inch baking dish.

2. In a single layer, line the baking dish with graham crackers, breaking crackers as necessary to fill the entire dish. Sprinkle, dollop, scatter, or top the crackers with the bananas. Top with another layer of crackers, working again to fill the whole dish.

3. In a medium saucepan, combine the butter and brown sugar, and bring to a boil over medium heat. Reduce the heat to low and cook for 3 minutes until thickened. Remove from the stovetop.

4. Stir the peanut butter, vanilla, and salt into the butter/sugar mixture, mixing until smooth.

5. Pour the delicious-smelling peanut butter mixture evenly over the top cracker layer.

6. Transfer to the oven and bake at 325°F until the mixture bubbles, caramelizes, and infiltrates the cracker layer with magic, about 20 minutes.

7. Cool completely, then cut into 24 squares. Store in an airtight container at room temperature for up to 3 days.

LEMON POPPY RIBBONS

Makes 24 cookies

I love a breakfast pastry in the morning (it reminds me of visiting my nonna), but I can't help but tinker. I mean, what if a breakfast pastry could be cookie dough based? Introducing these buttery, lightly sweet ribbons, which are based on a cookie recipe by Fannie Farmer (G.O.A.T.). They will definitely bring some sunshine to your breakfast table.

113g	unsalted butter, softened	1 stick (8 T)
75g	sugar	⅓ cup
20g	honey	1 T
1	large egg yolk	
3g	vanilla extract	¾ tsp
180g	flour	1¼ cups
8g	poppy seeds	2 tsp
2g	kosher salt	½ tsp
1 recipe	Microwave Lemon Curd (recipe follows)	
1 recipe	Lemon Poppy Glaze (recipe follows)	

1. Heat the oven to 350°F. Pan-spray or line two half-sheet pans with parchment paper or silicone baking mats.

2. In the bowl of a stand mixer fitted with the paddle attachment, cream together the butter, sugar, and honey on medium-high for 2 to 3 minutes until well combined. Scrape down the sides of the bowl with a spatula.

3. Add the egg yolk and vanilla and beat until smooth.

4. Add the flour, poppy seeds, and salt and paddle on low just until the dough comes together, no longer than 1 minute. Scrape down the sides of the bowl with a spatula.

5. Tip the dough out onto a clean work surface, divide into thirds, and roll each third into a 10-inch log. Carefully transfer the dough to the prepared baking pans spaced evenly apart, 2 logs on one of the pans, 1 log on the other.

6. With your thumb beginning just inside the end of one log, press down to form an indentation. Repeat almost all the way down the log to form a well down the center. Repeat with the remaining 2 logs.

7. Bake at 350°F until golden brown around the bottom edges of the logs, 8 to 10 minutes. Remove the pans from the oven and press a small spoon down the center of the logs to reinforce the cavity. Keep the oven on.

8. While the dough is still warm, spoon the lemon curd into the wells, dividing evenly among the 3 logs. Return to the oven and bake until the curd forms a skin and the cookie log tops are lightly golden, 5 more minutes.

9. Cool the cookies on the pans for 15 minutes.

10. Once cool, use a fork to drizzle the glaze over the logs. Allow the glaze to set for 15 more minutes. Use a thin knife to slice each log at an angle into 1-inch slices.

11. Transfer the cookies to a plate or an airtight container for storage. At room temperature, the cookies will keep fresh for 3 days; in the freezer, they will keep for 1 month.

(recipe continues)

MICROWAVE LEMON CURD

Makes 2½ cups

→ No microwave, no problem! Cook over medium heat on the stovetop and proceed as written.

200g	sugar	1 cup
2	large eggs	
2g	kosher salt	½ tsp
160g	lemon juice	⅔ cup (4 to 5 lemons)
113g	unsalted butter, cubed	1 stick (8 T) (divided)

1. In a microwave-safe medium bowl, whisk together the sugar, eggs, and salt. Add the lemon juice and whisk until smooth. Toss in 56g (4T) of butter.

2. Cook the curd in the microwave in 1-minute spurts, stirring after each, until smooth and until the curd thickens enough to coat the back of a spoon without running (4 to 6 minutes, depending on your microwave). Don't undercook it; the curd mixture will thicken a tad during the first 3 minutes and then truly thicken between 4 to 6 minutes.

3. Add the remaining 56g (4 T) of butter and stir to combine. If there is any sign of lumps, strain the mixture into a new bowl or container. Refrigerate to cool until ready for use.

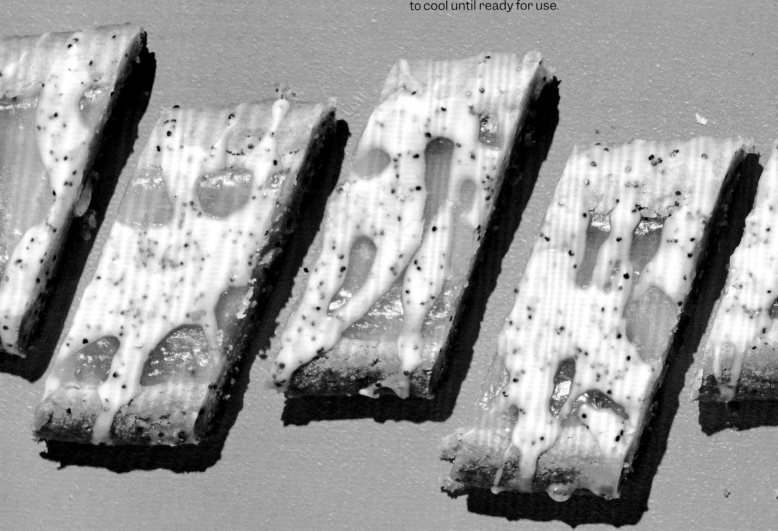

LEMON POPPY GLAZE

Makes ⅓ cup

60g	confectioners' sugar	½ cup
18g	lemon juice	1 T + 1 tsp
3g	poppy seeds	¾ tsp
	kosher salt	pinch

In a medium bowl, whisk together the confectioners' sugar, lemon juice, poppy seeds, and salt until lump-free.

HOT TIN ROOF COOKIE CAKE

Makes one 8-inch cake

I don't claim to be an expert on much, but when it comes to ice cream, I've done my 10,000 hours—mostly on the consumption side with some time in the pros. I've had just about every flavor on the market, from grocery aisle to boutique scoop shop, and I can expound for hours on butter content, variegates, and inclusions. So when someone mentioned a "Tin Roof" flavor during an R&D session and my mind drew a blank, I knew I needed to hear more. Tin Roof ice cream is a simple and winning combination of vanilla, chocolate sauce, and whole peanuts with mysterious origins and a die-hard fan base: sold! This cookie cake (see page 253)—a cookie larger than any cookie has ever been before and covered with fun—is a tribute to these flavors with a dreamy base, killer chocolate swirl, and classic chocolate peanut topping. We certainly won't be mad if you serve it à la mode in true Tin Roof fashion.

→ You can make the fudge ripple sauce in advance, but the chocolate-covered peanuts should be made just as you are ready to decorate the cake, allowing the peanuts to "glue" to the top as the chocolate cools. You'll want to account for extra time for your cookie cake decor to set before serving.

154g	unsalted butter, softened	11 T
200g	sugar	1 cup
70g	light brown sugar	⅓ cup (packed)
1	large egg	
8g	vanilla extract	2 tsp
190g	flour	1⅓ cups + more for dusting
4g	baking powder	1 tsp
4g	kosher salt	1 tsp
1 recipe	Fudge Ripple Sauce (recipe follows), cooled	
1 recipe	Chocolate-Covered Peanut Topping (recipe follows)	
2 or 3	salted roasted peanuts, for finishing	

1. In the bowl of a stand mixer fitted with the paddle attachment, cream together the butter, sugar, and brown sugar on medium-high for 2 to 3 minutes until well combined. Scrape down the sides of the bowl.

2. Add the egg and vanilla and beat until smooth.

3. Add the flour, baking powder, and salt and paddle on low just until the dough comes together, no longer than 1 minute. Scrape down the sides of the bowl with a spatula.

4. Tip the dough out onto a large piece of plastic wrap. Form it into a flat square, wrap, and refrigerate until chilled and firm, about 2 hours.

5. Use masking tape to secure a large piece of parchment to your work surface and dust it with flour.

6. Unwrap the chilled dough onto your rolling surface and roll the dough into a 9 × 13-inch rectangle.

7. Spread the cooled fudge ripple sauce across the dough from edge to edge. If the dough becomes too soft and begins to pull or rip, use the parchment paper to slide it onto a baking pan and chill for a few minutes before continuing.

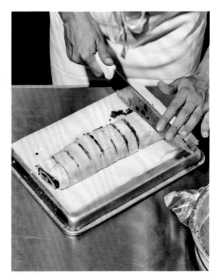
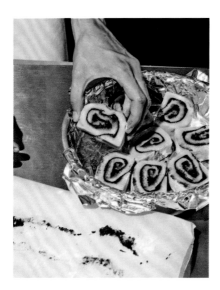

8. Beginning on a short side, roll up the dough jelly-roll style into a tight log. Lift the edge of the parchment closest to you as you roll to help the dough along as needed. Don't worry too much about cracks or fudge smudges as they will not be visible in the end!

9. Freeze the roll until firm enough to slice (but not frozen solid), about 20 minutes.

10. Heat the oven to 350°F. Line an 8-inch metal ring mold or cake pan with foil and coat with pan-spray. If using a ring, place on a baking sheet.

11. Transfer the semifrozen log to a cutting surface and slice into thirteen 1-inch rounds. Arrange the spiral rounds in the ring or cake pan with 1 piece at the center. It's okay if they don't touch, as they will melt and bake together in the oven.

12. Bake at 350°F until the edges of the cookie are puffed and the center looks dry, 18 to 20 minutes. It will deflate as it cools.

13. Allow the cookie cake to cool completely before unmolding. Transfer to a plate or cake stand.

14. Use a spoon to scoop the chocolate-covered peanut topping around the edge of the cookie cake. Use a Microplane to grate 2 or 3 peanuts over the topping. Allow 2 hours for the chocolate to set completely at room temperature.

(recipe continues)

FUDGE RIPPLE SAUCE

Makes about ½ cup

50g	sugar	¼ cup
20g	cocoa powder	¼ cup
2g	kosher salt	½ tsp
55g	heavy cream	¼ cup
28g	unsalted butter	2 T
8g	vanilla extract	1½ tsp

In a heavy-bottomed pot, stir together the sugar, cocoa powder, and salt. Add the heavy cream, butter, and vanilla and whisk together over medium heat until hot but not yet boiling. Transfer to a bowl and chill until cold, about 1½ hours.

CHOCOLATE-COVERED PEANUT TOPPING

Makes about ¾ cup

70g	salted roasted peanuts	½ cup
80g	milk chocolate chips	½ cup
2g	flaky salt	1 tsp

1. Heat the oven to 350°F. Line a half-sheet pan with parchment paper or a silicone baking mat.

2. Spread out the peanuts on the prepared sheet pan and retoast at 350°F until fragrant, about 10 minutes. (We like these extra toasty!) Let cool.

3. In a microwave-safe bowl, melt the milk chocolate chips in the microwave in 30-second spurts, stirring after each, until smooth.

4. Stir the toasted peanuts and flaky salt into the milk chocolate. Use immediately.

CHOCOLATE BABKA COOKIES

Makes 20 cookies

When it was time to get started on this book, I wanted to call in the biggest guns I knew for support, and I count my lucky stars that pastry wizard and longtime friend Zoë Kanan replied with a "Heck, yes!" Though she has spent some time in the Milk Bar kitchens, her POV on pastry is so different from mine, due in part to her Texas-Jewish upbringing in addition to her unbridled curiosity. When we kicked off our recipe planning, these babka cookies were at the top of her wish list and quickly became a favorite of mine. Flaky, chocolaty, with a flavor that will remind you of the buttery, bready side of babka (and absolutely stunning to behold), they are well worth the little extra elbow grease they take to produce. Just don't call 'em rugelach.

Another way Zoë and I differ: While I would personally pour on the glaze, Zoë loves them light on glaze or with no glaze at all! So you do you and glaze them as much or as little as you want.

→ This cookie has yeast in it for flavor, texture, and a different tenderness from most cookies. It needs a little time for that flavor to develop in the fridge and the texture to relax, so no shortcuts, babe!

65g	sugar	¼ cup + 1 T (divided)
21g	instant yeast	2¾ tsp (1 packet)
75g	warm water	⅓ cup
168g	unsalted butter, softened	12 T (divided)
140g	cream cheese, softened	4 oz + 2 T
360g	flour	2½ cups + more for dusting
4g	kosher salt	1 tsp
1 recipe	Chocolate Babka Filling (recipe follows)	
1 recipe	Glaze, optional (recipe follows)	

1. In a medium bowl, combine 13g (1T) sugar, yeast, and water and stir together with a fork. Some small lumps are okay and will dissolve naturally. Let sit until frothy, about 10 minutes.

2. In the bowl of a stand mixer fitted with the paddle attachment, cream together 140g (10T) butter, cream cheese, and 50g (1/4 cup) sugar on medium speed for 2 to 3 minutes until smooth.

3. Add the flour and salt and paddle on low speed until curds form but some dusty flour bits remain, about 30 seconds.

4. Still on low, pour the bloomed yeast mixture into the bowl and paddle to incorporate. Increase the speed to medium for 30 seconds to form a smooth and cohesive dough.

5. Tip the dough out onto a work surface and divide in half. Place each half onto a large piece of plastic wrap and pat into a flat square. Wrap and chill in the refrigerator for at least 2 hours and ideally overnight.

6. Heat the oven to 350°F. Pan-spray or line two half-sheet pans with parchment paper or silicone baking mats.

7. Use masking tape to secure or simply place a large piece of parchment on your work surface and dust it lightly with flour. Roll 1 piece of the dough into an 8 × 10-inch rectangle, the 8-inch side facing you, continuing to dust with flour as needed to keep it from sticking to the rolling surface.

(recipe continues)

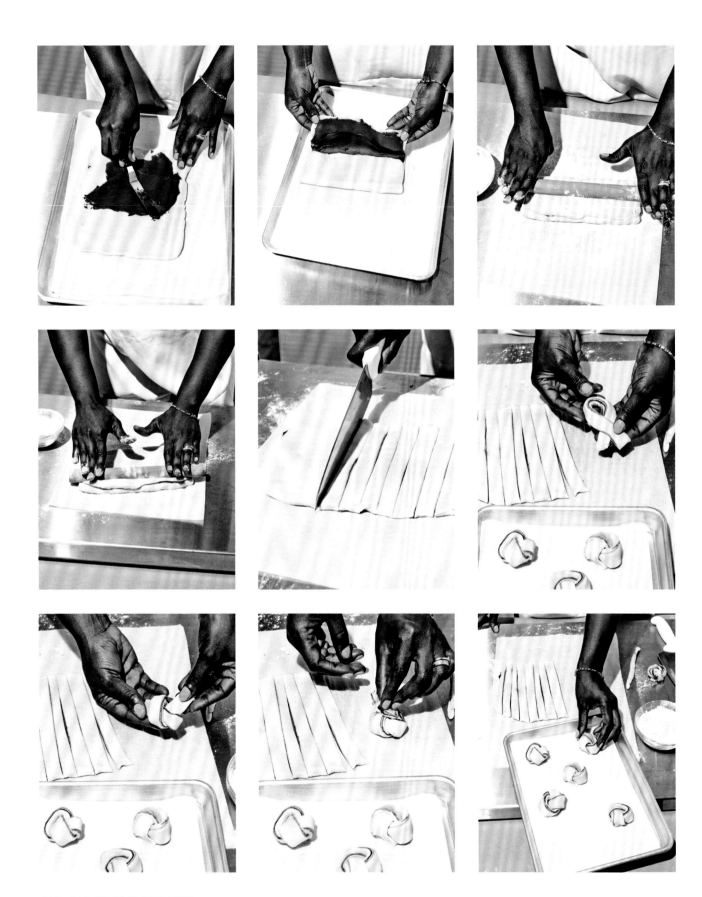

8. With the 8-inch side still facing you, fold the dough in thirds like a letter. Unfold the top third, the section farthest from you, and make a mark at the two-thirds point. Use an offset spatula or spoon to spread half (125g) of the chocolate filling over the two-thirds of the dough closest to you, leaving a small section of dough around the edge bare. The top one-third farthest from you should be bare.

9. Fold the dough like a letter again, beginning by folding the unfilled top third in first, then the bottom chocolate-filled third over to form alternating layers of dough and filling. If the dough feels warm or sticky after folding, transfer it to a half-sheet pan and chill for 10 minutes, until it begins to firm back up.

10. Re-roll the dough into an 8 × 10-inch rectangle, dusting lightly with flour to avoid sticking to the work surface.

11. With the 8-inch side still facing you, use a ruler and a pizza cutter or chef's knife to mark and cut the dough away from you bottom-to-top into strips ¾ inch wide. You should get 10 strips about 10 inches long.

12. Pick up 1 strip of dough and tie it into a simple knot by crossing the ends to form a loop in the middle and pulling one end through the loop. Pinch the ends together to fuse and place the cookie on the prepared pan with the pinched ends underneath. The thinner the strips, the easier they are to tie and fold. If you're having a hard time, try trimming down the strips' width slightly. Repeat with the remaining strips until all the cookies are formed.

13. Repeat the filling and rolling process with the second piece of dough or double wrap it and freeze for up to a month.

14. Bake the cookies at 350°F until they puff and open slightly to reveal stripes of filling and are firm to the touch with just a little color, 15 to 16 minutes.

15. Melt the remaining 28g (2T) butter, and immediately brush the still-hot cookies with it. Glaze while warm if that's your thing.

16. Transfer the cookies to a plate or an airtight container for storage. At room temperature, the cookies will keep fresh for 5 days; in the freezer, they will keep for 1 month.

CHOCOLATE BABKA FILLING
Makes 250g (1 cup)

128g	semisweet chocolate, chopped	¾ cup
42g	unsalted butter	3 T
60g	honey	3 T
6g	cocoa powder	1 T
1g	kosher salt	¼ tsp

1. In a medium microwave-safe bowl, melt the chocolate and butter in the microwave in 30-second spurts, stirring after each, until smooth.

2. Stir in the honey, cocoa powder, and salt, mixing until smooth. Set aside until cooled to room temperature and thickened.

GLAZE
Makes 150g (½ cup)

→ If you're going to go the glaze route, feel free to co-author this recipe: substitute in, say, coffee or chocolate milk in place of milk to give the glaze more individuality!

120g	confectioners' sugar	1 cup
30g	milk	2 T

In a small bowl, whisk together the confectioners' sugar and milk until smooth. Set aside until ready to use.

SPRINKLE COOKIE PIE CRUST

Makes two 9-inch pie shells

If you've had a slice of Milk Bar Pie, you may have noticed that the base is not a typical flaky pie dough. Nothing against the classic butter-flour combo, I just think we can bring more flavor to the pie table. While cookie crumb crusts (ah, have you been paying attention!?) or crumb crusts have long been my pie base move, I like to keep an open pastry mind. So what would WOW me at the base of, say, a strawberry ice cream pie (see page 78)? A creamy-dreamy vanilla cookie pie crust—basically one large cookie! This is a parbaked crust and is best used for no-bake fillings. Most anything cream-based would be killer.

→ Read up on clear vanilla extract and how its magic is different from that of its dark vanilla cousin on page 15.

→ Looking for a great filling for this great crust? I vote for this supereasy strawberry ice cream (page 78).

226g	unsalted butter	2 sticks (16 T)
250g	sugar	1¼ cups
1	large egg	
28g	clear vanilla extract	2 T + 1 tsp
340g	flour	2½ cups + more for dusting
8g	kosher salt	2 tsp
2g	baking powder	½ tsp
1g	baking soda	¼ tsp
50g	rainbow sprinkles	⅓ cup

1. In the bowl of a stand mixer fitted with the paddle attachment, cream together the butter and sugar on medium speed for 2 to 3 minutes until combined. Scrape down the sides of the bowl with a spatula.

2. Add the egg and vanilla and beat until smooth, about 1 minute.

3. Add the flour, salt, baking powder, and baking soda and paddle on low just until the dough comes together, no longer than 1 minute. Scrape down the sides of the bowl with a spatula.

4. Turn the dough out onto a work surface, lightly dusted with flour, divide into 2 equal pieces, and flatten into 2 evenly shaped pancakes. Roll each dough pancake out between two sheets of parchment paper to a rough 12-inch round circle, ½-inch thick. (Using parchment here is a real sanity saver, so don't skip it!) If you only plan to make one pie shell now, do not roll out the second pancake. Rather, double-wrap it in plastic and freeze it. Thaw before using.

5. Peel back the top parchment paper layer, scatter half of the sprinkles over one round, place the top parchment paper back down, and press the sprinkles gently into the dough with a light roll of the rolling pin. Slide the parchment paper patty onto a half sheet pan and refrigerate for 30 minutes. Repeat with the second dough pancake.

6. Heat the oven to 350°F and grease two 9-inch pie tins.

7. Remove the rolled dough from the fridge and allow to warm at room temperature 2 or 3 minutes until pliable, but still cold.

8. Peel back both pieces of parchment paper and transfer the dough, sprinkle-side up, to cover the pie tins. Use your fingers to press down the side and into the edges of the pan, ensuring the bottom is evenly covered in dough. If any tears or rips occur, tear off little pieces from the edge of the dough to patch as necessary. It will not be noticeable after baking!

(recipe continues)

9. Trim around the edge of the dough (scraps = snacks!), leaving 1 inch of overhang. Use the tips of your fingers to roll the overhang edge under and pinch so it rests on the lip of the pie tin. Use your thumb to crimp the crust edge or dip the tines of a fork in flour and press firmly all the way around. Freeze for 20 minutes to firm up. If making 2 pie shells, repeat with the second piece of dough.

10. Use 1 or 2 large pieces of foil to mold inside and over the crimped edge of the firm pie shell. Place onto a half-sheet pan and fill the cavity with baking beans or rice. (Pie weights are too heavy for this!)

11. Blind bake the shell at 350°F until it begins to turn opaque, 15 to 20 minutes. Carefully lift and remove the foil and finish baking until lightly golden throughout, for 5 to 7 more minutes.

12. Cool completely on a rack before filling.

3-INGREDIENT COOKIE PIE

Serves 8 to 10

When you don't have time to crush the epic Sprinkle Cookie Pie Crust (page 221), this very simple, creamy pie filled with flavored Cool Whip is clutch.

Or go all-in and fill the dang thing with ice cream, yielding an ice cream cookie pie (no one's mad at that!!). Or feel free to get fancy and use 2 cups of real whipped cream or a legit pastry cream, pudding, etc. I'm still not mad at it.

16-ish soft baked cookies, depending on size of pie dish and size of cookies

2 large spoonfuls of mix-in: jam, nut butter, caramel sauce, or drink powder (see page 150), or to taste

1 (8-ounce) tub Cool Whip

1. Cover a non-metal pie dish with a layer of cookies and microwave for 15 seconds to soften.

2. Press the cookies together with your hands to create a solid layer of cookie, making sure to work up the sides of the dish.

3. Scoop the mix-in of choice straight into the Cool Whip tub and mix to combine. If you're into a tie-dye vibe, feel free to leave this a little streaky.

4. Spoon your Cool Whip on top of the cookie crust layer and smooth it evenly with a spoon. Pop into the fridge to firm up for at least 1 hour before eating.

CRUNCHIES & CRISPIES

IF THERE'S ONE THING THAT I HAVE LEARNED IN MY DECADES (I'M
counting those grade school bake sessions!) of baking, it's that every person has their own baked good identity. Some folks go for chocolate over all else, others prefer fresh and fruity. Some might favor flaky textures, others live the Jell-O-y smooth life. The thought of warm baking spices—nutmeg, ginger, cardamom—sounds cozy to some and sends others running. These personalities resonate all the way down to baked-ness. I proudly identify as a soft and fudgy fiend. I like my baked treats as close to raw as the baking gods and my oven will allow, and—much to my mother's horror—I consider cookie dough a major food group. Why would you want something crispy and crunchy when you could have something ooey and gooey, I pondered.

As I've grown to be one part baker and one part business owner, I've had to make peace with the fact that not everyone eats the way I do, and we've made room at Milk Bar for all dessert POVs. I've watched as a tray of overbaked-to-me Compost Cookies got gobbled up by two prep cooks. I've seen the magic on someone's face as they bust open a Snap and discover the layers of texture and flavor within. And in full transparency: I, too, cannot be trusted with a pint of crunchy Bday Cake Crumbs.

This section is our tribute to all things crispy and crunchy … and also my confession that there is a time and place for well-baked baked goods. To be clear, creating a cookie that breaks apart in your hands but retains its flavor and integrity is no easy feat—it's not just a matter of keeping them in the oven longer. Developing these recipes meant deconstructing and then reconstructing everything we understood about the science of baking. Time, temperature, leaveners, water content: It's all a balancing act to get to that perfectly loud and proud creation. While gooey will always have my heart, I am certainly not mad at a confetti cookie that you can hear from outer space when you go in for a big bite.

GOLDEN OATIES

Makes 28 cookies

I have never been a proponent of overly ornate baked goods, half because I believe eating is a "close your eyes and take it in" experience and half because I'm far too impatient to spend the extra time on optics. You may look at the lacy, shiny crevices of these super-thin, buttery, caramelized stunners and think I spent hours crocheting to form an edible doily, but in reality they come together in a flash. With a coat of chocolate and a sprinkle of sea salt, they deliver big-time on the eyes-closed front as well.

→ This style of cookie is a big hit for Passover. Just swap out the flour for ½ cup matzo meal.

70g	butter	5 T
40g	rolled oats	½ cup
110g	light brown sugar	½ cup (packed)
90g	honey	¼ cup
50g	flour	⅓ cup
4g	kosher salt	1 tsp
90g	semisweet chocolate, chopped	½ cup
	flaky salt, for topping	

1. Heat the oven to 350°F. Pan-spray or line two half-sheet pans with parchment paper or silicone baking mats.

2. In a small saucepan, melt the butter over medium heat. Add the oats and toast until the butter begins to brown and the oats smell fragrant and take on a light golden color, about 3 minutes.

3. Add the brown sugar and honey and cook until just boiling throughout. Remove the pan from the heat and stir in the flour and kosher salt.

4. Immediately scoop teaspoons of the hot batter onto the prepared pans, 7 or 8 per pan. The batter will flatten into very thin discs, so space with a minimum of 4 inches in between them. If the batter sticks to the teaspoon, use a second small spoon to scoop it onto the pan.

5. Bake at 350°F until flat, bubbling throughout, and lightly caramelized, 8 to 10 minutes. Keep an eye on them as they can overcaramelize quickly. Transfer the pan to a cooling rack and use a knife to gently separate any cookies that flooded together.

6. Cool for 30 seconds or until you can slip the knife or a small offset spatula underneath the cookies. Working quickly, carefully lift and roll a cookie into a cigar shape. Transfer to a cooling rack to cool completely. Repeat the process for the remaining cookies. The unshaped cookies may need to be gently microwaved or warmed over the stove if they become unrollable.

7. In a microwave-safe medium bowl, melt the chocolate in the microwave in 30-second spurts, stirring after each, until smooth.

8. Dip one or both ends of each cookie into the melted chocolate and return to the cooling rack. Sprinkle flaky salt over the chocolate and leave to set for 1 hour.

9. Transfer the cookies to a plate or an airtight container for storage. At room temperature, the cookies will keep fresh for 3 days; in the freezer, they will keep for 1 month.

CRUNCHY CORN COOKIES

Makes 26 smallish cookies

Forever a fan of the salty-sweet tension, I count the corn cookie among my favorite Milk Bar treats. It's almost corn bread but with the sugar and butter levels cranked up to eleven, and it feels just like coloring outside the lines enough to bring adventure to the everyday. Those mad geniuses in the Milk Bar Lab bested themselves in my eyes when they cut this dough into triangles and used them as the base for the most killer dessert nachos I have ever encountered. If you want to nacho for yourself, I suggest pulling the Chewy Strawberry Caramel from page 182 and adding a crumb of your choosing on top! Otherwise enjoy these in circular form, solo!

→ These cookies bake slow and low for maximum crunch and minimum color. Gotta let that corny spirit shine!

→ If you've ever made my cereal milk from past cookbooks, you know the deal with freeze-dried corn and corn powder made from freeze-dried corn. If you need a little guidance, read more on page 14.

→ This dough is stickier than most—this allows the cookies to spread while the extra moisture evaporates during baking.

→ If you live in a very humid environment or these cookies aren't crunchy all the way through, bake them an additional 1 to 3 minutes to dry them out a bit more.

170g	unsalted butter, softened	1½ sticks (12 T)
165g	sugar	¾ cup + 1 T
1	large egg	
5g	water	1 tsp
180g	flour	1¼ cups
20g	corn powder	¼ cup
7.5g	cornstarch	1 T
4g	baking soda	1 tsp
3g	kosher salt	¾ tsp

1. Heat the oven to 275°F. Pan-spray or line two half-sheet pan with parchment paper or silicone baking mats.

2. In the bowl of a stand mixer fitted with the paddle attachment, cream together the butter and sugar on medium-high for 4 minutes until well combined. Scrape down the sides of the bowl and add the egg and water and mix for 4 more minutes.

3. Add the flour, corn powder, cornstarch, baking soda, and salt and paddle on low speed until just combined, about 20 seconds.

4. Scoop the dough into 1-tablespoon balls onto the prepared pans 3 to 4 inches apart. (These cookies spread!)

5. Bake at 275°F for 25 minutes. These cookies won't change color much, so make sure you set your timer. If they don't turn out as crispy as you would like, bake for 2 to 3 minutes longer next time.

6. Let the cookies cool briefly on the pans, then transfer to a cooling rack. Share immediately unless you have enviable self-control. If you do have cookies left over, store them in an airtight container for up to 1 week.

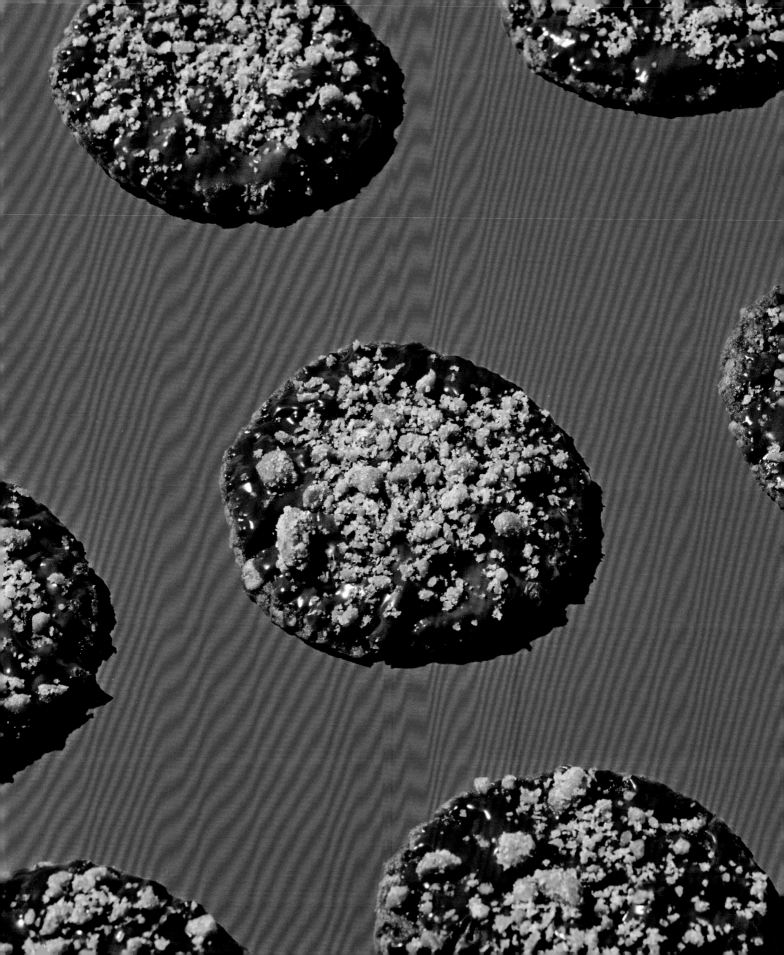

CHOCOLATE TOFFEE HOBNOBS

Makes 26 cookies

Aside from getting to see new sights and meet new people, the best part about traveling abroad is tearing up the aisles of the local grocery store in search of foods not sold in the US. Whenever life takes me to a new country, I beeline for the supermarket and load my cart up with whatever catches my eye. Nutella in every shape and form, chips (or crisps as the locals might say) in new and exotic flavors, candy bars with weird names and textures, and, of course, local cookies. This recipe is based on England's famous Hobnob cookies, which use oats to create a buttery, almost granola bar appeal. We cover them in chocolate and coat them with bits of toffee to plus up their otherwise wholesome existence.

75g	rolled oats	⅔ cup
113g	unsalted butter, softened	1 stick (8 T)
140g	sugar	⅔ cup
15g	honey	2 tsp
10g	whole milk	2 tsp
4g	vanilla extract	1 tsp
95g	flour	⅔ cup
4g	baking soda	1 tsp
4g	kosher salt	1 tsp
180g	semisweet chocolate, chopped	1 cup
10g	grapeseed oil	1 T
1 recipe	Toffee Bits (recipe follows)	

1. Heat the oven to 325°F. Pan-spray or line two half-sheet pans with parchment paper or silicone baking mats.

2. Pulse the oats in a food processor until broken up into a coarse meal.

3. In the bowl of a stand mixer fitted with the paddle attachment, cream together the butter, sugar, and honey on medium-high for 2 to 3 minutes until well combined Scrape down the sides of the bowl, add the oats, milk, and vanilla, and beat until smooth.

4. Add the flour, baking soda, and salt and paddle on low speed just until the dough comes together, no longer than 1 minute. Scrape down the sides of the bowl with a spatula.

5. Using a ½-ounce cookie scoop (or 1-tablespoon measure), scoop the dough onto the prepared pans 2 to 3 inches apart.

6. Bake at 325°F until flattened and evenly browned throughout, 15 to 17 minutes. Cool the cookies slightly on the pans.

7. In a microwave-safe medium bowl, melt the chocolate and oil in the microwave in 30-second spurts, stirring after each, until smooth.

8. Dip the top of each cookie into the melted chocolate. Lift and gently shake to allow any excess to drip off. Return to the sheet pan and repeat with the entire batch.

9. Sprinkle the crushed toffee bits over the top. Let the chocolate set for about 2 hours, cementing the toffee bits in place. Speed this up by popping the cookies in the fridge or freezer for 5 to 10 minutes.

10. Transfer the cookies to a plate or an airtight container for storage. At room temperature, the cookies will keep fresh for 3 days; in the freezer, they will keep for 1 month.

(recipe continues)

TOFFEE BITS

Makes ¼ cup

56g	unsalted butter	4 T
110g	light brown sugar	½ cup (packed)
2g	kosher salt	½ tsp

1. Line a half-sheet pan with parchment paper or a silicone baking mat.

2. In a saucepan, melt the butter over medium heat. Add the brown sugar and salt and whisk to combine.

3. Cook over medium heat, whisking constantly, until the mixture thoroughly boils, darkens to the color of peanut butter, and pulls away from the sides of the pan, about 5 minutes.

4. Pour the mixture onto the prepared pan and use a spatula to spread into an even layer. Let cool for 30 minutes.

5. Break the hardened toffee into shards. Transfer to a food processor or plastic bag and crush into pea-size bits.

CRUNCHY CORNFLAKE CHOCOLATE CHIP COOKIES

Makes 30 smallish cookies

Our classic cornflake chocolate chip cookie was originally born because someone left the cornflake crunch (page 159) in the oven too long and I thought, No biggie. We'll just hide it in a chocolate chip cookie dough—no one will ever know. Little did I know that everyone would WANT to know what the heck made those cookies so delicious—buttery and caramelized beyond anyone's expectations. You know I love to wonder what if. This cookie is that what-if moment—if making the cornflake crunch extra crunchy did that to the soft and fudgy cookie, what if I made the entire cookie extra crunchy? You're not going to be mad at the results.

→ These cookies bake slow and low for maximum crunch.

→ This dough is stickier than most—this allows the cookies to spread while the extra moisture evaporates during baking.

→ If you live in a very humid environment or these cookies aren't crunchy all the way through, bake them an additional 1 to 3 minutes to dry them out a bit more.

170g	unsalted butter, softened	1½ sticks (12 T)
85g	light brown sugar	¼ cup + 2 tablespoons (packed)
75g	sugar	¼ cup + 2 T
1	large egg	
8g	vanilla extract	1 tsp
180g	flour	1¼ cups
7.5g	cornstarch	1 T
4g	baking soda	1 tsp
3g	kosher salt	¾ tsp
150g	mini chocolate chips	¾ cup
45g	Frosted Flakes cereal	1 cup

1. Heat the oven to 275°F. Pan-spray or line two half-sheet pans with parchment paper or silicone baking mats.

2. In the bowl of a stand mixer fitted with the paddle attachment, cream together the butter, brown sugar, and sugar on medium-high for 4 minutes until well combined. Scrape down the sides of the bowl, add the egg and vanilla and mix for 4 minutes.

3. Add the flour, cornstarch, baking soda, and salt and paddle on low speed until just combined, about 20 seconds.

4. Paddle in the mini chocolate chips and Frosted Flakes and mix for 10 seconds until just combined.

5. Scoop the dough into 1-tablespoon balls onto the prepared pans 3 to 4 inches apart. (These cookies spread!)

6. Bake at 275°F for 25 minutes. These cookies won't change color much, so make sure you set your timer. If they don't turn out as crispy as you would like, bake for 2 to 3 minutes longer next time.

7. Let the cookies cool briefly on the pans, then transfer to a cooling rack. Share immediately unless you have enviable self-control. If you do have cookies left over, store them in an airtight container for up to 1 week.

CRUNCHY CONFETTI COOKIES

Makes 28 smallish cookies

If you've spent a summer day in New York City, you know the magic that is a cup of vanilla soft serve, absolutely coated in rainbow sprinkles, straight from the Mister Softee truck. Your adult brain tells your eyes that these colorful flecks aren't really bringing anything tastewise to the soirée, but one bite and you know the truth: Sprinkles are the key to happiness. Yes, they bring joy, but texturally, sprinkles improve all they touch by adding a layer of sweet crunch. In these confetti cookies gone crispy, the sprinkles are the star of the show.

→ Read up on clear vanilla extract and how its magic is different from that of its dark vanilla cousin on page 15.

→ These cookies bake slow and low for maximum crunch and minimal color to let those sprinkles shine.

→ Sprinkles, or jimmies, are not all created equal. Some are fat-based, some sugar-based. The ingredient list on the side will tell you which is which. Sugar-based sprinkles will crunch best here, but fat-based sprinkles will also do great work.

→ This dough is stickier than most—this allows the cookies to spread while the extra moisture evaporates during baking.

→ If you live in a very humid environment or these cookies aren't crunchy all the way through, bake them an additional 1 to 3 minutes to dry them out a bit more.

1. Heat the oven to 275°F. Pan-spray or line two half-sheet pans with parchment paper or silicone baking mats.

2. In the bowl of a stand mixer fitted with the paddle attachment, cream together the butter, sugar, and brown sugar on medium-high for 4 minutes until well combined. Scrape down the sides of the bowl, add the egg and vanilla, and mix for 4 minutes.

3. Add the flour, cornstarch, baking soda, and salt and paddle on low speed until just combined, about 20 seconds.

4. Add the rainbow sprinkles and mix for 10 more seconds.

5. Scoop the dough into 1-tablespoon balls onto the prepared pans 2 to 3 inches apart.

6. Bake at 275°F for 25 minutes. These cookies won't change color much, so make sure you set your timer. If they don't turn out as crispy as you would like, bake for 2 to 3 minutes longer next time.

7. Let the cookies cool briefly on the pans, then transfer to a cooling rack. Share immediately unless you have enviable self-control. If you do have cookies left over, store them in an airtight container on the counter for up to 1 week.

170g	unsalted butter, softened	1½ sticks (12 T)
115g	sugar	½ cup + 1 T
45g	light brown sugar	3 T
1	large egg	
4g	clear vanilla extract	1 tsp
215g	flour	1½ cups
7.5g	cornstarch	1 T
4g	baking soda	1 tsp
3g	kosher salt	¾ tsp
60g	rainbow sprinkles	⅓ cup

COMPOST ANIMAL CRACKERS

Makes 36 small cut-out cookies

In the early days of Milk Bar, we jumped at the chance to snag free travel in exchange for baking at events. We were gobsmacked that anyone would fork over airline tickets and hotel rooms in exchange for cookies and truffles, but who were we to say no?! When our friends at a fancy-pants fashion company asked us to come to Paris (!!!) to bake for their big fashion show, we renewed our passports and packed our bags. All that for making 6,000 compost animal crackers—pshhhh, how hard can it be?! Cut to some very cranky bakers in the basement of a French hotel, cursing the tiny chocolate chip, oat, graham cracker, and coffee—studded animals as we painstakingly cut them out one by one across 36 hours straight. The cookies were a hit and we did get to see the City of Lights eventually, but say "Merci" to your lucky stars that your compost cookie zoo is much smaller than ours.

→ For optimal animal cut-outs, the right cutter is key. Try searching online for "mini cookie cutters with spring ejection." Hilarious, I know, but it works!

226g	unsalted butter, softened	2 sticks (16 T)
115g	light brown sugar	½ cup (packed)
100g	sugar	½ cup
1	large egg	
1g	vanilla extract	¼ tsp
400g	flour	2¾ cups
4g	kosher salt	1 tsp
3g	baking powder	¾ tsp
1g	baking soda	¼ tsp
150g	mini chocolate chips	¾ cup
100g	mini butterscotch chips	½ cup
40g	graham cracker crumbs	⅓ cup
40g	rolled oats	½ cup
4g	ground coffee	1 T
50g	kettle-style potato chips	2 cups
50g	mini pretzels	1 cup

1. In the bowl of a stand mixer fitted with the paddle attachment, cream together the butter, brown sugar, and sugar on medium speed about 1 minute until smooth. Scrape down the sides of the bowl with a spatula. Add the egg and vanilla and beat for 7 to 8 minutes until well combined.

2. Add the flour, salt, baking powder, and baking soda and paddle on low speed until just combined, about 20 seconds.

3. Still on low speed, paddle in the mini chocolate and butterscotch chips, graham cracker crumbs, oats, and coffee just until incorporated, about 30 seconds. Still on low speed, paddle in the potato chips and pretzels until broken into small pieces.

4. Turn the dough out and flatten into 2 pancakes. Roll each dough pancake out between two sheets of parchment paper to a ¼-inch thickness. Using your cookie cutter, stamp creatures into the dough as close to one another as possible (do not remove the cookies). Refrigerate the entire sheet of dough for at least 30 minutes.

5. Heat the oven to 325°F. Pan-spray or line a sheet pan with parchment paper.

6. Pop your chilled zoo off the parchment and transfer them carefully to the prepared baking sheet, spacing them ¼ inch apart. Reshape your dough scraps into a ball and roll out anew. Stamp and refrigerate as above.

7. Bake the cookies until the edges are set and the center is no longer glossy, 6 to 8 minutes, depending on the size of your animals.

CHEESE PLATE COOKIES

Makes 40 cookies

In the eyes of some, a cheese plate is an acceptable dessert. No comment. While I like a stinky blue as much as the next gal, it's not what I want after I've crushed a massive plate of steak frites. I usually forgo the fromage for a slice of chocolate cake or a crème brûlée. But perhaps the cheese-course-as-dessert POV is just missing a bit of a bridge. Something that says, yes, this is cheese, but there's also something sweet here as well. These cookies are the ticket. They have caraway and rye to earn their almost-cracker keep, plus citrus and a coating of sugar to bring some fun.

2g	caraway seeds	¾ tsp
140g	sugar	⅔ cup
4g	grated orange zest	2 tsp
226g	unsalted butter, softened	2 sticks (16 T)
1	large egg	
180g	flour	1¼ cups
125g	medium rye flour	1¼ cups
6g	kosher salt	1½ tsp
50g	dried cranberries, chopped	⅓ cup
45g	turbinado sugar	¼ cup
4g	flaky salt	2 tsp

1. Line a 9 × 5-inch loaf pan with 2 large pieces of plastic wrap. Leave a few inches of overhang.

2. In a saucepan, toast the caraway seeds over medium heat, swirling regularly until they crackle and pop and smell fragrant, about 2 minutes.

3. In the bowl of a stand mixer fitted with the paddle attachment, paddle together the sugar and orange zest on medium-low for 2 minutes until combined. Add the butter and cream on medium-high for 2 to 3 minutes until well combined. Scrape down the sides of the bowl, add the egg, and beat until smooth.

4. Add the flour, rye flour, and kosher salt and paddle on low speed just until the dough comes together, no longer than 1 minute. Scrape down the sides of the bowl with a spatula.

5. Paddle in the chopped cranberries just until incorporated.

6. One handful at a time, press and mold the cookie dough into the pan to form a compact loaf. Fold the plastic overhang over the top and chill for at least 2 hours until firm.

7. Heat the oven to 350°F. Pan-spray or line two half-sheet pans with parchment paper or silicone baking mats.

8. On a plate, stir together the turbinado sugar and flaky salt. Remove the loaf of dough from the pan and brush the outside of the loaf with water. Press each side into the sugar/salt mixture to coat.

9. Use a long chef's knife to slice the loaf crosswise into the thinnest slices possible. Arrange the cookies on the pans as you go, as they soften quickly once sliced. If you only want to bake half the cookies at a time, double-wrap the remainder of the loaf with plastic wrap and freeze for later use.

10. Bake at 350°F until the cookies are completely crisp and lightly golden, 20 to 22 minutes.

11. Let the cookies cool briefly on the pans, then transfer to a plate or an airtight container for storage. At room temperature, the cookies will keep fresh for 3 days; in the freezer, they will keep for 1 month.

COOKIE COOKIES

Makes 12 cookies

I've never been one to chase trends. I'd much rather work head down, sleeves rolled up, chasing what's inside my own imagination and curiosity. But…I'm not blind. I scour the aisles of the grocery store and follow Instagram baking accounts, and every so often a food trend steals my attention. For example: the tiny pancake cereal craze of 2020. Tiny, adorable, golden pancakes made on a griddle and served in a bowl with milk. What is not to love?! This cookie reminds me that dessert can have a sense of humor, that there is room for personality and joy in even the smallest corners of your cookie cookbook.

Then, since I was thinking about breakfast, I remembered the grocery run many years ago where I FINALLY convinced my mom to buy me a box of Cookie Crisp. I was enamored with the idea of eating tiny cookies for breakfast, so that is one of my top ten food memories. So now I present to you: cookies that taste like cookies that taste like cereal.

→ These cookies bake slow and low for maximum crunch.

170g	unsalted butter, softened	1½ sticks (12 T)
175g	sugar	¾ cup + 2 T
1	large egg	
2g	vanilla extract	½ tsp
2g	water	½ tsp
145g	flour	1 cup
20g	cocoa powder	¼ cup
4g	kosher salt	1 tsp
6g	baking soda	1½ tsp
170g	chocolate chips	1 cup
55g	Cookie Crisp cereal	1½ cups

1. Heat the oven to 275°F. Pan-spray or line two half-sheet pans with parchment paper or silicone baking mats.

2. In the bowl of a stand mixer fitted with the paddle attachment, cream together the butter and sugar on medium-high for 2 to 3 minutes until well combined. Scrape down the sides of the bowl and add the egg, vanilla, and water and mix for 2 more minutes.

3. Add the flour, cocoa powder, salt, and baking soda and paddle on low speed until just combined, about 20 seconds.

4. Paddle in the chocolate chips and mix until well incorporated.

5. Scoop the dough into 1-tablespoon balls onto the prepared pans 3 to 4 inches apart. (These cookies spread!) Place 5 pieces of Cookie Crisp cereal on each scoop of dough. I place 1 on top and 4 all around on the sides of the small scoop.

6. Bake at 275°F for 25 minutes. These cookies won't change color much, so make sure you set your timer. If they don't turn out as crispy as you would like, bake for 2 to 3 minutes longer next time.

7. Let the cookies cool briefly on the pans, then transfer to a cooling rack. Share immediately unless you have enviable self-control. If you do have cookies left over, store them in an airtight container for up to 1 week.

BUTTERED TOAST COOKIES

Makes 12 cookies

In the more-is-more food world, buttered toast is kind of an anomaly. It could not be simpler or more plain Jane and yet it's highly craveable and deeply satisfying…so much so that most Americans keep a special kitchen device on their counters at all times just to make it! What other dish can make this claim? And what is toast's appeal? The crisp texture that only lasts a few moments, the richness of warmed butter, the simple heartiness. So we made a crisp cookie that uses toasted flour to bring that depth of flavor in and a pinch of butter on top pushes it right over the edge.

→ Like s'mores and steaks, everyone likes their toast cooked differently. Brown your butter and flour with your ideal toastiness in mind.

268g	unsalted butter	2 sticks (16 T) + 3 T, divided
215g	flour	1½ cups
150g	light brown sugar	⅔ cup (packed)
85g	sugar	⅓ cup + 1 T
1	large egg	
30g	water	2 T
6g	vanilla extract	1½ tsp
5g	kosher salt	1¼ tsp
4g	baking soda	1 tsp

1. In a heavy-bottomed saucepan over medium heat, cook 2 sticks (224g) of the butter, whisking occasionally. Cook until the butter darkens to a light toasty brown, 8 to 9 minutes.

2. Pour the brown butter into a shallow dish and chill in the fridge until solidified, about 1 hour.

3. Heat the oven to 400°F. Line two half-sheet pans with parchment paper.

4. Set one pan aside and spread the flour in an even layer on the other. Toast in the oven, stirring about 5 minutes in, until tanned throughout (the color of the flour will darken significantly once hydrated in the dough!), 10 to 12 minutes. Set aside to cool to room temperature.

5. Reduce the oven temperature to 350°F.

6. Use a large spoon to scoop the chilled brown butter into the bowl of a stand mixer fitted with the paddle attachment. Combine with the brown sugar and sugar, mixing on medium speed for 2 minutes until broken down and crumbly. Increase the speed to medium-high and beat for 5 minutes until light and creamy.

7. Scrape down the sides of the bowl with a spatula and add the egg, water, and vanilla. Beat on medium speed until smooth.

8. Add the toasted flour, salt, and baking soda and paddle on low speed just until the dough comes together, no longer than 1 minute. Scrape down the sides and bottom of the bowl with a spatula and mix for 10 more seconds to evenly combine.

9. Wipe down and re-line the half-sheet pan used to toast the flour with parchment paper. Using a 2-ounce cookie scoop (or a ¼-cup measure), scoop the dough onto the parchment-lined pans 3 inches apart.

10. Bake at 350°F until flattened and dry throughout, 14 to 16 minutes.

11. In a microwave-safe dish, melt the remaining 3 tablespoons butter in 10-second spurts until liquid. Brush the melted butter on top of the hot, just-baked cookies. The cookies will crisp as they cool.

12. Let the cookies cool briefly on the pans, then transfer to a plate or an airtight container for storage. At room temperature, the cookies will keep fresh for 5 days; in the freezer, they will keep for 1 month.

CRUNCHY BLUEBERRY & CREAM COOKIES

Makes 28 smallish cookies

Our blueberry-muffin-top-in-cookie-form takes on a new life in this crispy iteration. When I walk by a display case of muffins and see ones with especially caramelized tops, I can never resist. It's just so rule-breaky! Take it to the edge, I think! This fruity, creamy combo in all its crispness leads me to believe it's time muffins step aside as the breakfast of champs and make way for this breakout star.

→ These cookies bake slow and low for maximum crunch.

→ This dough is stickier than most—this allows the cookies to spread while the extra moisture evaporates during baking.

→ If you live in a very humid environment or these cookies aren't crunchy all the way through, bake them an additional 1 to 3 minutes to dry them out a bit more.

170g	unsalted butter, softened	1½ sticks (12 T)
115g	sugar	½ cup + 1 T
45g	light brown sugar	3 T (packed)
1	large egg	
5g	water	1 tsp
180g	flour	1¼ cups
7.5g	cornstarch	1 T
4g	baking soda	1 tsp
3g	kosher salt	¾ tsp
125g	white chocolate chips	¾ cup
80g	dried blueberries	½ cup

1. Heat the oven to 275°F. Pan-spray or line two half-sheet pans with parchment paper or silicone baking mats.

2. In the bowl of a stand mixer fitted with the paddle attachment, cream together the butter, sugar, and brown sugar on medium-high for 4 minutes until well combined. Scrape down the sides of the bowl. Add the egg and water and mix for 4 minutes.

3. Add the flour, cornstarch, baking soda, and salt and paddle on low speed until just combined, about 20 seconds.

4. Paddle in the white chocolate chips and dried blueberries, mixing for 10 seconds.

5. Scoop the dough into 1-tablespoon balls onto the prepared pans 3 to 4 inches apart. (These cookies spread!)

6. Bake at 275°F for 25 minutes. These cookies won't change color much, so make sure you set your timer. If they don't turn out as crispy as you would like, bake for 2 to 3 minutes longer next time.

7. Let the cookies cool briefly on the pans, then transfer to a cooling rack. Share immediately unless you have enviable self-control. If you do have cookies left over, store them in an airtight container for up to 1 week.

HOT HONEY GRAHAMS

Makes 30 to 40 crackers

The flavor ante has been raised significantly in the last few years as hot honey came on the scene. Drizzling this spicy, sticky, sweet magic brings anything—I'm talking fried chicken, roasted veggies, soup, pancakes—to the millionth level and is the secret ingredient in making these DIY graham crackers even more, more, more.

→ Roll it as thin as you think is possible. Then roll it thinner. Paper thin. It makes a huge difference!

→ Don't like it hot? Skip the red pepper flakes, triple the cinnamon, and proceed with the recipe as usual for original graham cracker goodness.

15g	apple cider vinegar	1 T
1g	red pepper flakes	¾ tsp
90g	honey	¼ cup
250g	sugar	1¼ cups, divided
127g	unsalted butter, softened	1 stick (8 T) + 1 T
12g	vanilla extract	1 T
215g	flour	1½ cups
7g	kosher salt	1¾ tsp, divided
4g	baking soda	1 tsp
1g	ground cinnamon	½ tsp

1. In a small saucepan, combine the vinegar and pepper flakes. Add the honey, bring to a simmer over medium heat, and cook for 2 minutes. (A 60-second blast in the microwave also does the trick.) Cool to room temperature.

2. Heat the oven to 325°F. Pan-spray two half-sheet pans and line with parchment paper.

3. In the bowl of a stand mixer fitted with the paddle attachment, cream together 150g (¾ cup) of the sugar, the butter, vanilla, and cooled honey mixture on medium-high for 2 to 3 minutes until well combined. Scrape down the sides of the bowl, add the flour, 6g (1½ teaspoons) of the salt, the baking soda, and cinnamon and paddle on low speed for 30 seconds or until no dry spots remain and a soft dough forms.

4. Scrape the dough onto a clean work surface and divide in half. Place each half between two sheets of parchment paper and use your hands to flatten into a square for ease of rolling. Using a rolling pin, roll out each piece of dough as thinly and evenly as possible, until around 1 inch shy of the dimensions of the half-sheet pan, about 17 × 12 inches. The dough should be paper thin. Chill for 10 minutes.

5. Carefully peel off the top piece of parchment paper. Use the prongs of a fork to pierce the sheet of dough (in the pastry world we call this docking) about 20 times all over.

6. Bake until medium brown (they will take on a lot of color!) and dry throughout, 15 to 20 minutes.

7. Working quickly, use a small cookie cutter to punch out as many cookies as possible from the still-hot cracker sheet, working outward in. It will become brittle as it cools and more challenging to punch, so make fast moves. (Using a pizza cutter or knife to cut a 2 × 3-inch grid also works.) Allow the crackers to cool completely.

8. In a large bowl or large zip-seal bag, mix together the remaining 100g (½ cup) sugar and 1g (¼ teaspoon) salt.

9. Gently toss the crackers in the sugar/salt mixture to coat completely. Transfer the crackers to a plate or an airtight container for storage. At room temperature, the crackers will keep fresh for 7 days; in the freezer, they will keep for 1 month.

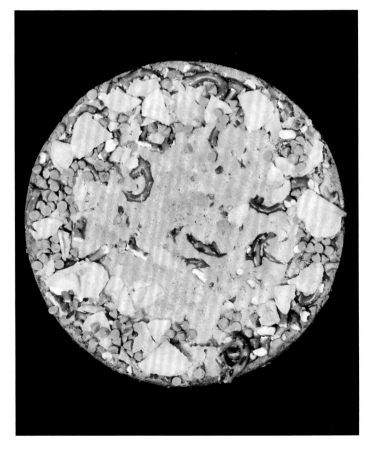

BUILDING A COOKIE CAKE

AS THE PERSON WHO IS OFTEN CALLED TO SUPPLY THE CAKE for every celebration—birthdays, weddings, retirement parties, you name it—I fully appreciate that not every person is a cake person. In fact, for most of my life I was a proud member of the "no cake for me" club. Nothing against cake, I've come to make my peace with it obviously, but I just prefer the fudgy, warm gooeyness of a cookie. So when I'm tasked with celebrating a fellow non-cake lover, I turn to the hilarity that is the cookie cake. You can't help but be transported back to the mall food court at the mere mention of its name. Over the years at Milk Bar, we have learned to take those humble beginnings to new heights—we even have stations at our flagships where you can play "baker for a day" and create your own cookie cake combo. Here's how we get after it.

HOW TO BUILD A COOKIE CAKE

Step 1: Heat the oven to 350°F. Pan-spray an 8-inch cake ring or springform mold. Place on top of a pan-sprayed half-sheet pan.

Step 2: Decide on a cookie dough base (see pages 256 and 257). This is the color and flavor palette that will be the foundation of your creation. Mix the dough.

Step 3: Choose 1 to 3 mix-ins (see Our Favorite Mix-Ins, below) and add ¼ cup of each to the bowl. Think about your flavor story here—every cookie cake has a point of view. Salty-sweet? Chocoholic? B-day bonanza? You're the boss.

Step 4: Paddle on low in the mixer for 45 seconds until all mix-ins are evenly distributed throughout the dough.

Step 5: Flatten the cookie dough out into the ring evenly, making sure there are no divots and the mix-ins are visible throughout.

Step 6: Sprinkle additional mix-ins along the outer ¼ inch of the dough's edge, just inside the ring.

Step 7: Bake at 350°F until the cookie is caramelized, the outer edges are set, and the bull's-eye center has gained color and is barely glossy, 20 to 22 minutes.

Step 8: Cool the cookie cake completely before unmolding from the ring. Decorate to your heart's content—see below for our tips.

Step 9: Serve whole or slice into 8 wedges. At room temperature, the cookies will keep fresh for 3 days; in the freezer, they will keep for 1 month.

OUR FAVORITE MIX-INS:

Chocolate chips
Butterscotch chips
Potato chips
Mini pretzels
White chocolate chips
Dried blueberries
Mini marshmallows
Sprinkles
Pie Crumbs (page 119)
Cornflake Crunch (page 159)

A FEW COOKIE CAKE COMBOS FOR INSPIRATION:

Corn cookie base + dried blueberries + sprinkles
Chocolate cookie base + pretzels + butterscotch chips
Sugar cookie base + cornflake crunch + white chocolate chips
Vanilla cookie base + chocolate chips + mini marshmallows

COOKIE CAKE BASE

SUGAR BUILD-A-COOKIE BASE

Makes one 8-inch cookie cake

84g	unsalted butter, softened	6 T
70g	sugar	⅓ cup + 2 tsp
70g	light brown sugar	⅓ cup (packed)
1	large egg	
190g	flour	1⅓ cups
12g	milk powder	2 T
4g	kosher salt	1 tsp
1g	baking powder	¼ tsp
0.75g	baking soda	⅛ tsp

1. In the bowl of a stand mixer fitted with the paddle attachment, cream together the butter, sugar, and brown sugar on medium-high for 7 minutes. Scrape down the sides of the bowl.

2. Add the egg and beat until smooth, about 1 minute.

3. Add the flour, milk powder, salt, baking powder, and baking soda and paddle on low speed just until the dough comes together, no longer than 1 minute. Scrape down the sides of the bowl with a spatula. Your dough is ready to be made into a cookie cake (see How to Build a Cookie Cake, page 254).

VANILLA BUILD-A-COOKIE BASE

Makes one 8-inch cookie cake

84g	unsalted butter, softened	6 T
113g	sugar	½ cup + 1 T
55g	light brown sugar	¼ cup (packed)
1	large egg	
1g	vanilla extract	¼ tsp
170g	flour	1 cup + 3 T
18g	milk powder	3 T
4g	kosher salt	1 tsp
1g	baking powder	¼ tsp
0.75g	baking soda	⅛ tsp

1. In the bowl of a stand mixer fitted with the paddle attachment, cream together the butter, sugar, and brown sugar on medium-high for 7 minutes. Scrape down the sides of the bowl.

2. Add the egg and vanilla extract and beat until smooth.

3. Add the flour, milk powder, salt, baking powder, and baking soda and paddle on low speed just until the dough comes together, no longer than 1 minute. Scrape down the sides of the bowl with a spatula. Your dough is ready to be made into a cookie cake (see How to Build a Cookie Cake, page 254).

CORN
BUILD-A-COOKIE BASE

Makes one 8-inch cookie cake

113g	unsalted butter, softened	1 stick (8 T)
175g	sugar	¾ cup + 2 T
1	large egg	
110g	flour	¾ cup
40g	corn powder	½ cup
25g	corn flour	3 T + 2 tsp
4g	kosher salt	1 tsp
1g	baking powder	¼ tsp
0.75g	baking soda	⅛ tsp

1. In the bowl of a stand mixer fitted with the paddle attachment, cream together the butter and sugar on medium-high for 7 minutes. Scrape down the sides of the bowl.

2. Add the egg and beat until smooth, about 1 minute.

3. Add the flour, corn powder, corn flour, salt, baking powder, and baking soda and paddle on low speed just until the dough comes together, no longer than 1 minute. Scrape down the sides of the bowl with a spatula. Your dough is ready to be made into a cookie cake (see How to Build a Cookie Cake, page 254).

CHOCOLATE
BUILD-A-COOKIE BASE

Makes one 8-inch cookie cake

98g	unsalted butter, softened	7 T
150g	sugar	¾ cup
45g	light brown sugar	3 T
1	large egg	
1g	vanilla extract	¼ tsp
25g	dark chocolate chips	3 T
120g	flour	¾ cup + 1 T
35g	cocoa powder	⅓ cup + 1 T
4g	kosher salt	1 tsp
1g	baking powder	¼ tsp
1g	baking soda	¼ tsp

1. In the bowl of a stand mixer fitted with the paddle attachment, cream together the butter, sugar, and brown sugar on medium-high for 7 minutes. Scrape down the sides of the bowl.

2. Add the egg and vanilla and beat until smooth, about 1 minute.

3. In a microwave-safe medium bowl, melt the dark chocolate chips in the microwave in 30-second spurts, stirring after each, until smooth. Add to the mixer bowl and mix to combine.

4. Add the flour, cocoa powder, salt, baking powder, and baking soda and paddle on low speed just until the dough comes together, no longer than 1 minute. Scrape down the sides of the bowl with a spatula. Your dough is ready to be made into a cookie cake (see How to Build a Cookie Cake, page 254).

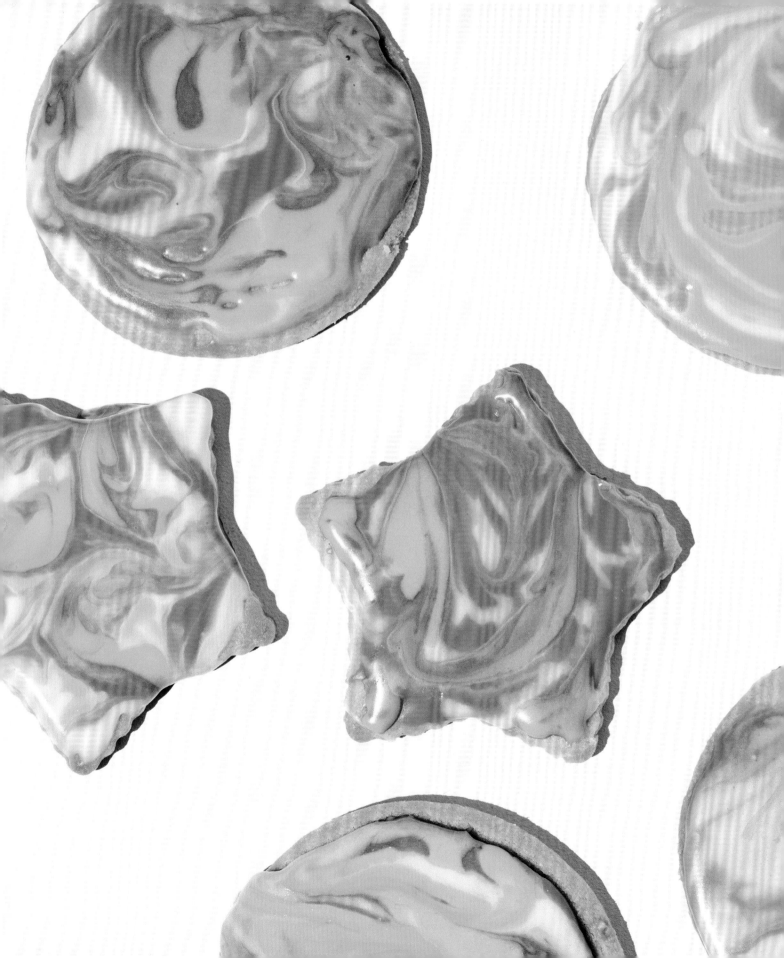

CUT-OUT COOKIES & GO-TO GLAZES

WHEN THE IDEA CAME TO LAUNCH A DIGITAL-ONLY, COME-AS-you-are, imperfectly perfect Bake Club on Instagram, I knew the first recipe had to check some boxes:

- supes easy
- tasty results
- few ingredients required
- maximum opportunity for creativity and personality

There was only one clear winner in my mind: Cut-Out Cookies!

No matter your kitchen savvy, cut-out cookies are a guaranteed win. First of all, making and decorating these things is a primo holiday time or celebratory activity. The definition of a "more than the sum of its parts" creation, a cut-out cookie gives infinite room for flavor and personality. Choose a brilliant cut-out cookie base, mix, chill, roll, cut, bake. Then buckle your seatbelt because when they come out of the oven in all kinds of shapes, the fun really begins as the glazes, jimmies, and sprinkles start to fly. Though any of the cut-out (aka wafer cookie) recipes from the Snaps chapter (page 160) will do, the Caramelized Wafers (page 183) are my family's go-to.

CUT-OUT COOKIE TIPS

- Start with a good base. The cookie doughs from the Snaps chapter work great: Chocolate Wafers (page 179), Caramelized Wafers (page 183), Cinnamon Donut Wafers (page 175), Pie Wafers (page 186), and PB Wafers (page 193).

- If you don't have cookie cutters, shape the dough into 2 logs, each 2 inches in diameter, cover, and refrigerate for 1 hour or more. Slice into ¼-inch-thick rounds, arrange on a greased or lined baking sheet, and bake.

- If you have rolling-pin anxiety, shape the dough into 2 logs, each just a bit larger in diameter than your preferred cookie cutter. Cover and refrigerate the logs for 1 hour or more, then slice into ¼-inch-thick rounds and use the cookie cutter to cut out a shape from each round. Place on a greased or lined baking sheet and bake.

- Trust me (I have nearly two decades of dough-rolling experience under my belt) when I say roll your dough out at room temperature between two sheets of parchment paper rather than on a floured countertop. The sanity saved is worth the extra item on the grocery list.

- Refrigerate or freeze your parchment paper sheet of cut dough to firm up, then pop the shapes out, place them on your greased or lined baking sheets, and repeat. Your cut-out cookie game just got a WHOLE lot stronger (and simpler).

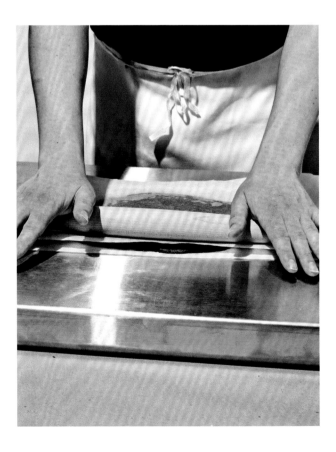

THE GLAZE FORMULA
(FLAVOR IT TO YOUR HEART'S CONTENT)

I had no doubt in my mind that Bake Club would be able to crush a killer batch of cut-out cookies, but what I was not expecting was the brilliance they brought to the choose-your-own-adventure glazing. I gave a simple formula for a solid glaze consistency (below) and turned the home bakers loose in their pantries in search of flavorful liquids to use. Check out Possible Glaze Liquids (below) to see some of the inspired selections they made.

60g	confectioners' sugar	½ cup
	liquid (see possible glaze liquids below)	1 T
	food coloring (optional)	

1. In a small bowl, combine the confectioners' sugar with the liquid and whisk until smooth. Add a drop or two of food coloring, if desired, and whisk again.

2. Gauge your glaze's consistency. If you want your glaze to be thicker, whisk in more confectioners' sugar. If you want your glaze to be thinner and looser, whisk in a splash more liquid. Every liquid and every kitchen has different hydration and humidity factors that contribute to your glaze's consistency.

3. Glaze and decorate the cookies using one of the glazing techniques (page 262). Then let the finished cookies rest until the glaze is set, 1 to 2 hours, before eating, serving, or packing up to share.

POSSIBLE GLAZE LIQUIDS

- Orange juice
- Lemonade
- Flavored coffee creamer
- Green tea
- Root beer

- Bitter liqueurs
- Carrot juice
- Grape jelly
- Maple syrup
- Raspberry puree (strained)

- Peanut butter + a splash of milk
- Chocolate syrup + a splash of milk
- Cream cheese + cinnamon + a splash of milk

- Milk + a splash of mint extract
- Stout beer
- Strawberry milk

GLAZING TECHNIQUES

LINE AND FLOOD

Transfer your glaze to a zip-seal sandwich bag. Close the bag, leaving a tiny opening, and press out the air, smooshing the glaze toward one corner. Zip the rest of the top shut. Use scissors to cut the tip of the corner off, creating a small opening for the glaze. Gently squeeze the bag to trace a solid line of glaze around the edges of your cut-out to create a border, then go back and fill in the center of the cookie with the glaze. The border will keep the glaze from spilling over the edges. Gently tap the cookie on the counter to help the glaze coat.

This works especially well if the glaze in the zip-seal bag is thick enough to pipe a line (add more confectioners' sugar to your glaze if yours is too runny to do that).

TIE-DYE

For the best tie-dye results, you'll need three different colored glazes. Spoon 2 teaspoons of color 1 glaze onto the center of a small plate. Drizzle 2 teaspoons each of the color 2 and color 3 glazes on top. Using a wooden toothpick, slightly swirl the colors together. Dip the top of a cookie into the multicolored glaze; let the excess drip back onto the plate. Using a toothpick, swirl the colors together on the cookie's surface.

This works especially well if the glaze is a pourable, thick-ish consistency. Add a splash more liquid if your glaze is too thick.

DUNK AND SPRINKLE

Fill one bowl with glaze and a second bowl or ridged plate with your favorite decor items: sprinkles, colored sugar, nonpareils, broken-up candy canes, etc. Holding your cookie by the edges, dunk the top of the cookie into the bowl of glaze, swirling it around quickly to ensure a smooth coating. Then quickly and carefully dip the glazed layer into the second bowl of toppings, pressing slightly so they adhere.

This works especially well if the glaze is a pourable, thick-ish consistency. Add a splash more liquid if your glaze is too thick.

PIPE AND DRIZZLE

Transfer your glaze to a zip-seal sandwich bag. Close the bag, leaving a tiny opening, and press out the air, smooshing the glaze toward one corner. Zip the rest of the top shut. Use scissors to cut the tip of the corner off, creating a small opening for the glaze. With your glaze as your paint, let your inner artist out, creating polka dots, zigzags, tiger stripes, you name it.

This works especially well if the glaze in the zip-seal bag is thick enough to pipe a line (add more confectioners' sugar to your glaze if yours is too runny to do that).

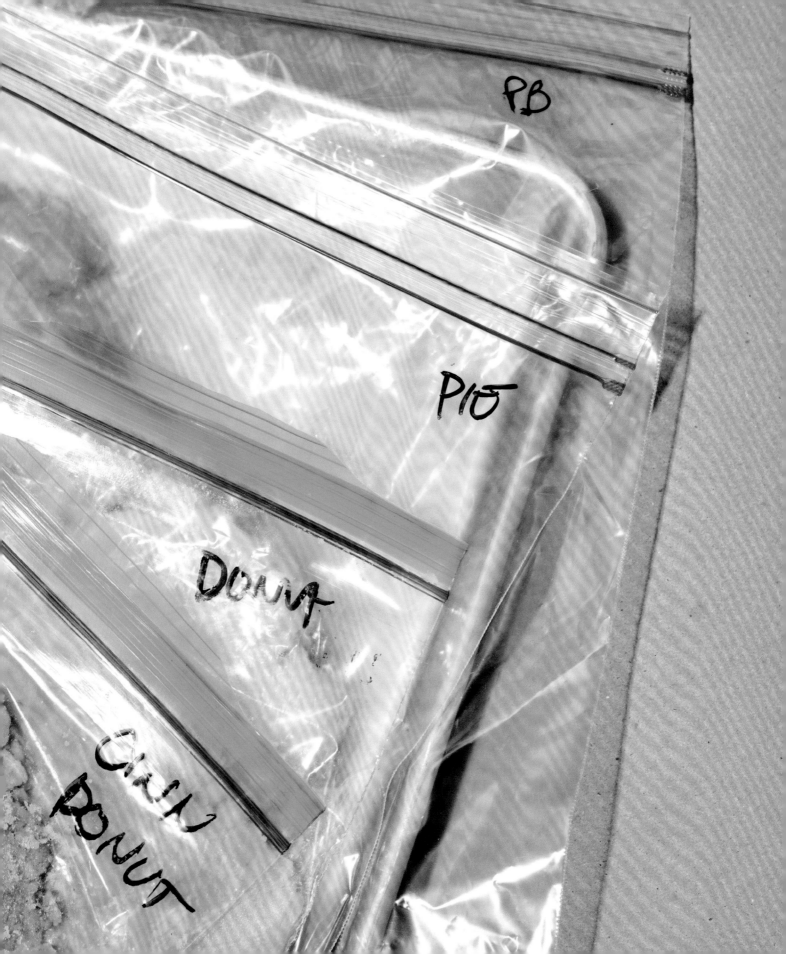

ACKNOWLEDGMENTS

Just when I thought I was the only one crazy enough to crush another cookbook assignment, I found my most loyal friends and partners at my side yet again, ready to climb cookie dough mountain.

Shannon Salzano, we would be lost without your brilliant eye, dry humor, silly voices, meticulous organization, journalistic word prowess, unstoppably can-do attitude, and killer taste. I'm pretty sure that makes you a Septuple Threat…

Jena Derman, she's all business, she's all party, she's on a red-eye, she's gearing up her motorcycle, she's solid wiggling all over town. And she's got twelve zip-seal baggies of cookies for me to taste, too. She's ride-or-die, babaaaay.

Zoë Kanan, from her first NYC job at nineteen to now, her brilliance brought a voice and lens to these pages that I'm incredibly wowed by and grateful for.

Francis Lam, our editor, our king. The details guy to our cookie pie. Thank you for always saying YES! when we say AGAIN?!

Ian Dingman, our brilliant designer, who brought these pages to life.

Erica Gelbard, the promo queen, **Chloe Aryeh,** the marketing maven, and **Kim Kaminsky,** our unstoppable PR Goddess, for making sure every book has the perfect home kitchen to inspire.

Kim Witherspoon, life guide, book agent. Thirteen years ago, who'da thought we'd still have words to fill the page?!

Henry Hargreaves, the brilliant eye behind the lens. Coach! Your calm, kind demeanor is the perfect balance to our crazy bakery mentality. You read us, and our cookies, like no one else. Thank you for bringing our work to life. Also, thank you, Rana!

Alex Watkins, for the beginning, the middle, and the end. We are so excited to cheer you onto your next adventure!

Abena Anim-Somuah (aka Beans!) for the brilliant recipe testing and friendship.

Cherese Derman for your killer eye and style.

Hilly O'Hanlon and the entire Milk Bar team, from photo shoots to cookie swaps and the most important just-because moments. You show up and show out every single time. You remind me daily of the superpowers a single cookie can hold and the ability a single idea can unlock. I could not imagine a better group of humans to have the privilege to spend my life showing up for.

To my unofficial creative directors and taste testers: **Laura Wagstaff, Sarabeth Turner,** and my most unimpressed and harshest critics: **Iris and Charlotte Morrison.** Thank you for keeping me fueled and humble.

To my family: **Will, Frankie, and Butter.** My last cookbook, promise! (That is, until the next one… 😊)

INDEX

Published in the United States by Clarkson Potter/Publishers, an imprint of Random House, a division of Penguin Random House LLC, New York.
ClarksonPotter.com
RandomHouseBooks.com

Library of Congress Cataloging-in-Publication Data
Names: Tosi, Christina, author. | Hargreaves, Henry, photographer. Title: All about cookies / Christina Tosi ; [photographs by Henry . Hargreaves]. Description: New York : Clarkson Potter, [2022] | Includes index. | Identifiers: LCCN 2021061789 (print) | LCCN 2021061790 (ebook) | ISBN 9780593231975 (hardcover) | ISBN 9780593231982 (ebook) Subjects: LCSH: Cookies. | Baking. | LCGFT: Cookbooks. Classification: LCC TX772 .T67 2022 (print) | LCC TX772 (ebook) | DDC 641.86/54—dc23/eng/20211231
LC record available at https://lccn.loc.gov/2021061789
LC ebook record available at https://lccn.loc.gov/2021061790.

ISBN 978-0-593-23197-5
Ebook ISBN 978-0-593-23198-2

Printed in China

Photographer: Henry Hargreaves
Editor: Francis Lam
Editorial Assistant: Darian Keels
Contributing Editor: Paige Resnick
Designer: Ian Dingman
Production Editor: Patricia Shaw
Production Manager: Phil Leung
Compositors: Merri Ann Morrell and Hannah Hunt
Copy Editor: Kate Slate
Indexer: Elizabeth T. Parson
Marketer: Chloe Aryeh
Publicist: Erica Gelbard
Book and Cover Design: Ian Dingman

10 9 8 7 6 5 4 3 2 1

First Edition

CHRISTINA TOSI is the two-time James Beard Award—winning chef and owner of Milk Bar, with locations in New York City, Toronto, Los Angeles, Boston, Las Vegas, and Washington, D.C. She was also a judge on Fox's *MasterChef Junior* series, was featured on the hit Netflix docu-series *Chef's Table: Pastry,* and hosts the Netflix series *Bake Squad.* She is the author of *Momofuku Milk Bar, Milk Bar Life, All About Cake, Milk Bar: Kids Only, Dessert Can Save the World,* and, for children, *Every Cake Has a Story.*

Clarkson Potter/Publishers
New York
ClarksonPotter.com

Cover design: Ian Dingman
Cover photographs: Harry Hargreaves

31901069071506